With 200 illustrations, 191 in color

Diana Ketcham with Michael R. Corbett, Mitchell Schwarzer, and Aaron Betsky
Principal Photography by Mark Darley

the de Young in the 21st century

a museum by Herzog & de Meuron

Thames & Hudson

Fine Arts Museums of San Francisco

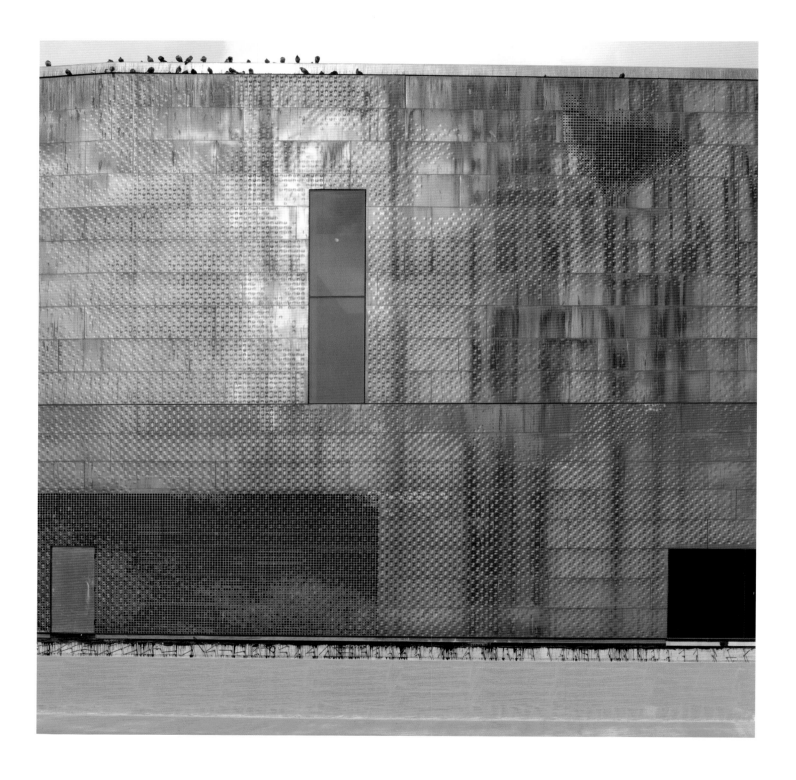

Photograph credits:

© Corporation of the Fine Arts Museums, Herzog & de Meuron,
Primary Designers, and Fong & Chan Architects, Principal Architects,
Mark Darley, Photographer: 1–9, 12, 14, 82 bottom, 109, 111, 112,
114–137, 149, 154–155, 156–196

© Corporation of the Fine Arts Museums, Herzog & de Meuron,
Primary Designers, and Fong & Chan Architects, Principal Architects:
52–53, 59 top, 82 top, 86, 88, 89, 90, 93, 94–95, 97, 98–99, 100, 101,
102, 103, 105, 106–107, 108

Hood Design: 138, 139, 140–141, 142, 144–145, 146, 147

Tobias Madörin / © Herzog & de Meuron: 61, 70

Joseph McDonald: 38

© Nacàsa & Partners: 81

© Margherita Spiluttini: 58, 60, 63 top (portraits), 67, 71, 72, 73, 74,
75, 76, 77, 78, 79, 80

© Kaz Tsuruta: 41, 43, 44, 45, 46, 50–51, 56–57, 91

Published on the occasion of the re-opening of the de Young
in Golden Gate Park, San Francisco, California, October 2005

Published with the assistance of the Ednah Root Foundation

First published in 2005 in hardcover in the United States of America by
Thames & Hudson Inc., 500 Fifth Avenue, New York, New York 10110

thamesandhudsonusa.com

Library of Congress Catalog Card Number 2005923735

ISBN-13: 978-0-500-34215-2
ISBN-10: 0-500-34215-6

Printed and bound in China

Wilsey Court, with Gerhard Richter's *Strontium* (2004), composed of 130
C-print photographs mounted on aluminum. Foundation purchase, gift
of Diane B. Wilsey, President, Board of Trustees, Fine Arts Museums of
San Francisco, on the occasion of the opening of the new de Young on
October 15, 2005, in memory of Alfred S. Wilsey, 2004.6

STATEMENT FROM THE PRESIDENT OF THE BOARD

Diane B. Wilsey

I was asked to become the Capital Campaign Chairman of the Campaign to Rebuild the de Young Museum in 1995. The de Young museum building was the property of the city of San Francisco, the city owned the land, and the city owned the collections. It was only reasonable to assume that the building, which had been damaged by the Loma Prieta earthquake in 1989, would be replaced with funds from a city bond issue. The majority of the money would be public money, and approximately $35 million to $45 million would need to be raised privately.

The vote on that bond issue occurred in November of 1996. To my surprise, it failed to attain the two-thirds majority necessary to win a general obligation bond. We tried another bond issue in June 1998 but, once again, by a very small margin, the required two-thirds majority of votes was not realized, and the city's funds were not made available to care for its damaged building or to protect its valuable art collections.

It was at this time that I decided not to undertake another bond issue, which I had learned could be fraught with unrelated political agendas and result in undeserved defeat. The day after the June bond issue failed, I told our director, Harry Parker, that I intended to raise the money to build the de Young privately. After a lengthy selection process, we chose a Swiss architectural firm—Herzog & de Meuron—who produced a spectacular but somewhat controversial design. Fong & Chan Architects were engaged as the architects of record and to prepare the working drawings. We chose Oakland landscape architect Walter Hood to complement the building with his designs. Then began a series of public meetings that involved hundreds of citizens, neighborhood groups, the Board of Supervisors, the mayor, and almost every elected official in San Francisco. Many of these meetings were contentious, some were constructive, and all required patience, humor, and humility. Eventually we prevailed, and work on the new de Young began.

The private fundraising goal was first set at $135 million and later increased to $165 million. To date $180 million has been raised from more than 7,000 donors. More than 4,000 donors who have contributed $1,000 each will be listed alphabetically on our donor wall on the west side of the entry court.

Many other trustees and friends have been very generous and creative in their gifts to the new museum. I have been encouraged throughout this project by the dedication, loyalty, and generosity of our volunteers, members, staff, and the community who truly want to see the museum restored. These people have made my job a pleasure, even in the darkest moments, and I am grateful to all of them.

DIRECTOR'S FOREWORD

Harry S. Parker III

The story of how the de Young museum came to have this stunning new home is a very different one from that of the many museums that embarked on building programs in the 1990s. In San Francisco, as in other cities, museums considered a change in location as a strategy for improving their situations. The Asian Art Museum was contemplating a move from Golden Gate Park to what was considered a more favorable location downtown. The San Francisco Museum of Modern Art wished to move from shared space in the Civic Center to a building of its own in the South of Market art zone.

For the de Young, however, a new building was not a policy option but a mandate—delivered by the civic engineer who appeared in my office seventeen years ago, during my first week as director, in fact. He reported that the existing museum was in danger of collapse during an earthquake, with the possibility of significant loss of life. It was then that the likelihood of building a new de Young began to influence all of our thinking about the future. When the museum was struck by the Loma Prieta earthquake in 1989, the seriousness of the damage made this likelihood a necessity.

What I am most appreciative of today is how the Board of Trustees was able to make an opportunity out of the engineer's grim pronouncements. The fact that so many people were excited by the promise of a completely new

building has given us a chance to reinvent the de Young. Planning for this building has sparked the expansion of the museum's collections, the broadening of its public appeal, and great improvement in its visitor services. The prospect of enhanced facilities for the collections attracted major gifts, among them the Dorothy and George Saxe Collection of Contemporary Craft in 1994. Another significant consequence was the acquisition of important pieces from Marcia and John Friede's collection of New Guinea art. The Phyllis Wattis Purchase Fund, along with the generosity of the Friedes, brought these first works. They were followed by the promised gift of a substantial number of works from the Friede's Jolika Collection, which dominates the exhibition of Oceanic art in the new building and allows the museum to claim representation of New Guinea art unsurpassed by any other museum in the United States.

Mrs. Wattis's gift also secured the great eighth-century Maya stela for the galleries of art of ancient America. The recent purchase of major African works through the Fund carries on her legacy. In addition, the Wattis family acquired the twelfth-century Dogon ancestor figure for the museum in her memory.

In the expansion of the collections of American paintings, sculpture, and decorative arts at the de Young during previous decades, the art of the post–World War II era was

View of the de Young from the Spreckels Temple of Music

neglected. That period now has become a focus of donations and purchases, many of them by longtime friends of the de Young. The Wattis gift has also permitted the acquisition of major American works, including the Ed Ruscha archive and his painting *A Particular Kind of Heaven,* a Richard Diebenkorn painting from the Ocean Park series, a de Kooning drawing, and a David Smith sculpture. Nan Tucker McEvoy, the granddaughter of the museum's founder, Michael de Young, provided funds for the purchase of an important de Kooning painting, *Untitled XX.* Bernard and Barbro Osher initiated a sculpture garden and collected numerous works by international artists such as Barbara Hepworth, Isamu Noguchi, and Claes Oldenburg and Coosje van Bruggen.

The potential for state-of-the-art facilities encouraged us to expand the treatment of textile arts, adding areas for conservation, study, and exhibition. Our plans for the textile space attracted hundreds of new gifts, particularly from George and Marie Hecksher, and led to the renaming of the department as the Caroline and H. McCoy Jones Department of Textile Arts.

As construction of the building began, it became clear that certain locations cried out for large-scale works that did not exist in our collection. We took the architectural opportunities of the new space as an occasion to invite leading contemporary artists to create work for the de Young. A mural by Gerhard Richter, commissioned by Dede Wilsey in memory of Alfred S. Wilsey; an installation by Andy Goldsworthy, the gift of Lonna and Marshall Wais; the Osher commission of a James Turrell Skyspace; and a Kiki Smith sculpture commissioned through the Dorothy and George Saxe Endowment Fund and the Friends of New Art—all forecast a commitment to exhibiting international contemporary artists that will grow stronger in the future. These site-specific works give substance to the Board of Trustees' announcement in 1990 that it would bring the collections up to the present. In addition to all this, Nancy B. and Jake L. Hamon have given the Education Tower, which will be the new icon of the de Young.

This book records and celebrates the story of the de Young and the complex interactions that brought us to a new museum for a new century. Diana Ketcham and her co-authors Michael R. Corbett and Mitchell Schwarzer, along with Aaron Betsky's interview with Jacques Herzog and Mark Darley's photography, bring to life the past and the process through which Herzog & de Meuron, Fong & Chan Architects, and landscape architect Walter Hood met the challenge of creating this building in harmony with its park setting.

The effort to create the new de Young involved many

people, but none of it would have succeeded without Dede Wilsey and the generous donors she enlisted in the new de Young campaign. The construction process was overseen by a distinguished building committee, chaired by Steven MacGregor Read and including T. Robert Burke, Charles Crocker, Belva Davis, J. Burgess Jamieson, Sylvia Kingsley, Diane B. Lloyd-Butler, George Marcus, Nan Tucker McEvoy, J. Alec Merriam, Barbro Osher, and Diane B. Wilsey. I would also like to express my personal appreciation to Deborah Frieden for her consistent and responsible management of the entire building process. Of course, a project of this scope involves more individuals than we could mention, but a listing of the primary participants, together with the board and staff, appears as an appendix to this volume. We are fortunate that so many individuals responded to the opportunity that lay in the responsibility to build a new, seismically safe de Young.

Looking back, we can see how the external challenge of a construction project had the effect of energizing donors, engaging artists, and redirecting collecting policies. Herzog & de Meuron were integral at every stage. They not only contributed an innovative and distinctive design for the new de Young, but they also participated in the reinvention process, lifting our horizons and forming new connections among the eclectic and fascinating de Young collections.

A HISTORY OF THE DE YOUNG AND ITS BUILDINGS

Michael R. Corbett

The de Young is San Francisco's oldest and largest art museum. A public institution belonging to the city, it has been a physical presence in Golden Gate Park since the end of the nineteenth century. Its colorful history, like San Francisco's, was shaped by bold individuals and calamities of nature, notably the earthquakes that imperiled the museum's buildings during its first century. The new de Young, designed by Herzog & de Meuron and opened in the fall of 2005, replaced a compound of six buildings constructed between 1916 and 1955. Historically, it is the successor of the museum established on the same site on 21 March 1895. In the beginning the museum was called, simply, the Memorial Museum, commemorating the California Midwinter International Exposition of January to July 1894, which had been a great popular and financial success for the city during depressed economic times.[1] The driving force behind both the museum and the exposition was Michael H. de Young (1849–1925), publisher of the *San Francisco Chronicle*, who took his inspiration from the Chicago World's Columbian Exposition of 1893. As director general of the San Francisco exposition, it was de Young who proposed, when the fair closed, to use the profits to establish a museum in the fair's Fine Arts Building.

The San Francisco Midwinter Exposition had been planned, designed, and built in only six months, in the midst of a depression, a feat that "everybody said . . . could not be done."[2] Following an unsolicited plan by Leopold Bonet, the official architect, A. Page Brown, planned five major buildings around a central court with an iron observation tower in a protected area of the park called Concert Valley.[3]

The first home of the Memorial Museum, the Fine Arts Building, was in the Egyptian Revival style, which had been popular fifty years before but was unusual in 1894. As a guide to the exposition described it:

Museum founder Michael H. de Young (1849–1925), publisher of the *San Francisco Chronicle* and the driving force behind the California Midwinter International Exposition of 1894

The first home of the de Young museum was the Egyptian
Revival–style Fine Arts Building (1894) designed by architect Charles
C. McDougall for the California Midwinter International Exposition
in Golden Gate Park. Photograph by Isaiah West Taber, 1894

The columns on the main building are an exact copy of those found in the ruins of the temple of Karnak at ancient Thebes, the capitals being suggestive of the lotus flower. Those on the sides of the vestibule are from the temple of Edfu, . . . and those in front from the temple of Luxor, . . . the subjects being exact reproductions of those found in the temples. The hieroglyphics accompanying each figure explain its meaning minutely to the Egyptologist.[4]

Designed by San Francisco architect Charles C. McDougall,[5] the Fine Arts Building was hailed by the *San Francisco Chronicle* as the "boldest and most original design"[6] among the exposition buildings: a brick structure, fifty feet high, with seventeen-inch walls coated in decorative plaster and a skylit roof supported by iron trusses. When it became a museum, its space was increased by building a rear annex and by moving to its south side the elaborately decorated Royal Bavarian Pavilion, with rooms reproduced from King Ludwig of Bavaria's famous palace, originally created by a team of prominent German designers for the Chicago exposition. Behind the museum was a residence for the curator in the exposition's Canadian Pavilion. Moved to the site, it was a wood, staff, and stucco structure in the style of a stone and half-timbered lodge.

Concert Valley in Golden Gate Park, June 1893. Two hundred undeveloped acres in the 1,000-acre park were selected by M. H. de Young for the Midwinter Exposition.

The decision to hold an exposition in San Francisco, as well as the selection of the site and designs, had been undertaken very quickly. In mid-July 1893, a call for proposals went out to local artists, architects, and engineers. By 6 August 1893, the submitted designs were displayed downtown in the Mills Building for viewing by the public, at a charge of twenty-five cents. The original approval for construction in Golden Gate Park by the board of park and recreation commissioners was made with the condition that the structures be temporary, specifically that they be dismantled within ninety days after the exposition closed. All but the brick Fine Arts Building were of wood and stucco construction. Permanent construction for the Fine Arts Building was debated up until the last minute, with park commission chairman W. W. Stowe objecting that the cost would divert money from the fair, and, more importantly, that buildings were inappropriate in the park, which was intended to be a retreat from the city.[7]

The 1894 Midwinter Exposition, inspired by the 1893 World's Columbian Exposition in Chicago, was planned and built in only six months.

The Grand Concourse at the Midwinter Exposition; the excavated site is today's Music Concourse. The Fine Arts Building (out of view) was across the drive at the lower right, and the new de Young museum occupies the place of the domed Horticultural and Agricultural Building (right). The 266-foot Bonet Electrical Tower was inspired by the 1889 Eiffel Tower. Photograph by Isaiah West Taber, 1894

Unity of architectural style was not the objective in San Francisco as it had been at the Chicago World's Columbian Exposition. Instead, the designers attempted a unity of atmosphere, achieved in part by the coloring of the buildings, and in part by the festivity and fantasy implied by the improbable combination of revival styles. With the major buildings drawing on Egyptian, Spanish, Moorish, Mission, Gothic, and Romanesque sources,[8] the total effect was intended to be more suitable to San Francisco, with its international population, than the architecture of the Chicago fair, which was based on precedents from ancient Rome and Renaissance Europe. The Fine Arts Building, in particular, with its freely interpreted Egyptian imagery, made an exotic contribution that added to the atmosphere of fantasy. Visitors entered "a square colonnade . . . surmounted by the inner sides of a finished pyramid, with lights in the very apex," sixty feet above. The columns, skylights, and other decorative detail were colored in bright reds, yellows, greens, and blues, producing a "weird and enchanting" effect.[9] Beyond the vestibule was a two-story skylit statuary court, with cove cornices of lotus leaves under a decorative railing.

This approach to style was not merely an expression of Victorian eccentricity. According to the *Official History*

Most of the exposition buildings were demolished when the fair ended, leaving the Fine Arts Building and the Royal Bavarian Pavilion (left), which was moved to this site to increase space for the Memorial Museum established by de Young in 1895.

of the exposition, the planners of the Midwinter Fair, working in haste, feared that imitations of other buildings, especially of the classical structures at the Columbian Exposition, would be compared unfavorably to their models.[10] The results won the approval of critic Edwards Roberts of the *Overland Monthly,* who wrote at the time of the fair's opening:

> I should be inclined to doubt the desirability
> of housing the Fine Arts in an Egyptian Temple,

but the building, per se, has many commendable features. As a bit of architecture it is most effective, and its situation, slightly above the level of the driveway around the Court, adds greatly to the impression of size and massiveness.[11]

A MUSEUM IN GOLDEN GATE PARK

From the outset, a permanent museum in Golden Gate Park was a subject of debate. Even the proposal to hold the

The Fine Arts Building featured a two-story skylit gallery. Photograph by Isaiah West Taber, 1894

elsewhere because it was "untypical of the rural landscape represented by a park."[12]

Following a proposal by Olmsted on the need for parks in San Francisco, Golden Gate Park was begun in 1868 with the city's purchase of a rectangular strip of 1,013 acres, much of it sand dunes, its western end bordering the Pacific Ocean. In 1871, William Hammond Hall presented a plan based on Olmsted's Central Park and launched its development, which was carried out by superintendent John McLaren from 1887 to 1943. Hall's original plan proposed only two buildings in the park, the Manor House and the Large Pavilion. Nevertheless, even before the 1894 exposition, a scattering of buildings had been constructed. Among the first were the Park Lodge, an administrator's office, in 1874; the Conservatory in 1878; and the Casino restaurant and observation tower in 1881. These were followed by the Sharon Building, containing a small natural history museum; the Carousel; the Sweeney Observatory; a series of music stands; and Park (now McLaren) Lodge, a new park headquarters and superintendent's residence built in 1895. The next century saw the construction of the Dutch Windmill in 1902, the first building of the California Academy of Sciences in 1916, the Beach Chalet in 1921, and Kezar Stadium in 1925.

THE MEMORIAL MUSEUM

After the Midwinter Exposition closed in 1894, Michael de Young struggled with the park commissioners to prevent the dismantling of the Fine Arts Building and to allow a permanent museum in the park. The notion of locating a museum in Golden Gate Park was not new, but "had often been agitated in the press"[13] before the fair opened. Despite their assertions to the contrary, it seems likely that de Young and others were hoping to establish a museum when they first argued for constructing the Fine Arts Building in brick. Once a brick building was erected, the battle to

exposition in the park had elicited strong opposition. Like advocates for urban parks in other American cities, many proponents of the park in San Francisco believed that its function as a refuge from the city could be best realized if buildings were excluded, according to historian Terence Young. The two leading proponents of parks in San Francisco, Frederick Law Olmsted, a commanding figure in American landscape architecture and the designer of New York's Central Park, and William Hammond Hall, designer of Golden Gate Park, are described as believing that "museums and athletics each had their role in life, but not in a park"; a museum was an urban amenity best located

The square "Egyptian" entry court of the Fine Arts Building was surmounted by a pyramid and decorated in bright red, yellow, green, and blue. Photograph by Isaiah West Taber, 1894

Opposite top: When the Memorial Museum opened, the two sphinxes at the entrance were joined by an eleven-foot bronze vase by Gustave Doré, *Poème de la vigne* (1877–78). The vase was sent from France and exhibited first at the Chicago World's Columbian Exposition in 1893 and then at the San Francisco Midwinter

keep it was partly won. For the same reasons the park commissioners had initially resisted holding the fair in the park, they now tried to keep the museum out.

De Young countered by arguing: "Every great museum in the world is in a park. In Central Park in New York, the great Metropolitan Museum is on one side and the Museum of Natural History on the other." He also cited the examples of Paris, where the Louvre stands at the east end of the Tuileries Gardens, and London, where the South Kensington Museum (now called the Victoria and Albert Museum) bordered Kensington Gardens.[14]

De Young's ownership of the *San Francisco Chronicle* and his political connections helped to generate support for his position, which ultimately prevailed. Surplus exposition funds were used to adapt the building for museum use. Around the pair of sphinxes at the entry, de Young planted Dracanea palm trees and a eucalyptus, known to later generations as the museum's "cornerstones." As it does now, the museum faced the Music Concourse, which was a transformation of the exposition's Grand Court and retained its pattern of paths and parterres. The Japanese Tea Garden, also a legacy of the fair, remained beyond the northwest corner, where it stands today, adjacent to the de Young's sculpture garden.

The earthquake of 18 April 1906 seriously damaged the museum. Photographs of the exterior show fallen plaster, and collapsed side-wall columns and upper wall areas. The museum was closed for a year and half for repairs; afterward its brick side walls were left exposed, without the Egyptian-style decorative stucco that originally covered them.

When the Memorial Museum had first opened in 1895, it housed neither an art collection nor a natural history collection per se, but a diverse mixture of art and artifacts. In addition to twenty-seven boxes of "curios" de Young had purchased in Europe, there were objects from the exposition, and others from the natural history collection

Exposition in 1894, after which it was bought by de Young from the French foundry that had cast it. Doré had died in 1883, leaving his casting bill unpaid.

Above: Damage from the 18 April 1906 San Francisco earthquake is visible along the top of the wall, where decorative plaster collapsed. The Royal Bavarian Pavilion, on the left, shows diagonal cracks characteristic of earthquake damage.

A HISTORY OF THE DE YOUNG

The staff of the Memorial Museum, c. 1910

previously shown at the park's Sharon Building. The displays included a picture gallery; a statuary hall; the work of women artists; relics of Alaska and the South Sea islands; relics of California history; medieval armor, swords, forgings and castings, locks and keys, stirrups, door knockers, strong boxes, and tapestries; jewels; Greek pottery; American Indian objects, especially from California; coins; musical instruments; ship models; American colonial utensils and implements of daily life; and an Egyptian mummy. Rooms were devoted to Napoleon, Germany, and a Colonial kitchen. The displays of natural history included more than 23,000 stuffed animals, birds, and eggs; and California products, such as "soil, cereals, nuts and fruits."[15]

During its formation and early growth, the museum's collection was under the enthusiastic, but amateur, guidance of Michael H. de Young, assisted by a series of curators. The first was Charles P. Wilcomb, a pioneer in the study of California Indian material whose work predated that of Alfred Kroeber and others more often credited in this field.[16] One reason for the initial resistance to the museum in the park was fear that it might fail, in part because there was no adequate collection to show. But as de Young stated at the opening, "We do not claim today to offer for your criticism a great, full-fledged museum . . . it was determined to create a nucleus of what someday would be a great museum."[17] Given de Young's vision of a municipal museum to educate the general public, the quality of its collections in natural history, California history, and the American Indian material was respectable. Over the next twenty years, de Young traveled the world, building up his own collections and soliciting donations of others. By 1916, he was claiming that the museum owned more than 1 million objects.

These objects were housed in a complex of buildings whose atmosphere had more in common with an exposition or a holiday destination than with the art museums of its time. Its name referred to a memorable event in the history of public entertainment and boosterism in San Francisco, the Midwinter Exposition of 1894, rather than a benefactor or an art movement, as was more common. At the opening, de Young stated, "In years to come this building will remind our people that in the midst of almost unprecedented financial depression, an industrial exposition was here projected and carried to a successful termination."[18]

AMERICAN MUSEUM BUILDINGS

The development of the M. H. de Young Memorial Museum occurred during one of the great periods of museum growth in the United States, the late nineteenth and early twentieth centuries. While its origins are in many ways a colorful and distinctively San Francisco story, it cannot be fully understood apart from the American museums of its time. Although museums were built in the United States before the Civil War, the museum only began to emerge as a widespread building type during the 1870s. Architecturally, the American museum from 1870 through the 1880s was varied in character. The Smithsonian Institution (1855) was castlelike, and the first Boston Museum of Fine Arts (1876), the Pennsylvania Academy of the Fine Arts in Philadelphia (1876), and the first Metropolitan Museum of Art in New York (1880) were designed in the High Victorian Gothic style. Beginning in 1893 there was a huge expansion in art-museum construction that came to an end with the Depression and World War II. A second, extended boom in museum building began in the 1960s and has continued to the present day.

Except for its architectural style, the de Young was a representative product of the first expansion period. Common to this era were the museums' origins in world's fairs or expositions, their location in urban parks, and their grand, classically inspired architecture. Their architecture was ambitious, but the collections were often weak or unfocused. Although most exposition buildings were of temporary construction, it was common for one fair structure to be built of permanent fireproof materials. Such a building was a secure place to house works of art during the fair and could remain as the fair's legacy after it closed. This was the case at the Centennial Exposition of 1876 in Philadelphia, which left its art museum, Memorial Hall, and the World's Columbian Exposition, which left its Fine Arts Building, now the Museum of Science and Industry. The Paris Exposition of 1900 left the Grand Palais and the Petit Palais, and the Louisiana Purchase Exposition of 1904 in St. Louis left its Fine Arts Building, now the St. Louis Art Museum.[19]

Subsequently, American museums of the period 1893 to 1932 overwhelmingly followed Beaux-Arts models in plan and classical precedents in style. The Art Institute of Chicago (1893), the first major addition to the Metropolitan Museum of Art in New York (1895), the second Museum of Fine Arts in Boston (1909), the Cleveland Museum of Art (1916), and the National Gallery of Art in Washington, D.C. (1941) are among the best-known examples. In the early twentieth century, a few art museums adopted styles with regional associations. The Spanish Colonial Revival–inspired de Young addition of 1916 fits within this group, which includes the Spanish Colonial Revival Fine Arts Building (1926) in San Diego, the Georgian Revival Fogg Art Museum (1927) at Harvard University, and the Spanish Colonial Revival Walker Art Center (1928) in Minneapolis.

THE M. H. DE YOUNG MEMORIAL MUSEUM

In San Francisco, the museum's Egyptian-style Fine Arts Building, the Renaissance- and Baroque-inspired Royal Bavarian Pavilion, and the half-timbered Canadian Pavilion presented a hodgepodge of images and an awkward juxtaposition of interior exhibit spaces. The unfocused collection and the visually unrelated architecture were manifestations of both the enthusiasm and the absence of restraint that had made it possible for de Young to create the museum in the first place.

From its inception, Michael de Young was a masterful promoter of the museum as well as its chief donor. When he gave talks, which were often quoted at length in the *Chronicle*, de Young spoke engagingly about himself and the museum. He would describe how his own collecting began with an interest in stuffed birds, or recount his adventures on a worldwide search for knives and forks. While de Young was able to draw in the general public with displays of childlike enthusiasm, he also knew how to use sophisticated arguments to encourage donations from the wealthy. He never failed to mention the recreational and educational functions of a museum, citing recreation as a reason for having the museum in the park rather than in the Civic Center or elsewhere in the downtown—an issue that would arise again in the 1990s when the museum had to be rebuilt.

Toward the end of his tenure, Michael de Young wished to increase the capacity of the museum beyond the buildings that had survived the 1906 earthquake. In 1916, when he was sixty-six, he proposed an Egyptian-style addition that would harmonize with the existing building. He was quickly persuaded to withdraw this scheme in favor of a style that was more Californian in spirit and reminiscent of the Panama-Pacific International Exposition (PPIE), which had just closed. Its rationale, which gained support once de Young abandoned his first plans, was asserting a distinctive identity for the region and the state of California. This aim appealed to business and civic leaders such as Joseph R. Knowland, the influential publisher of the *Oakland Tribune*, who supported the 1916

influential houses drew on various sources but were expressive of their place in California. His public buildings were boldly original yet rooted in traditional imagery. As a young man, he worked for some of the best-known architects in America: H. H. Richardson; Shepley, Rutan & Coolidge, Richardson's successor firm; and Henry Ives Cobb. He had been involved in the successful design of the Fisheries Building at the World's Columbian Exposition in Chicago in 1893, and in planning for the Louisiana Purchase Exposition in St. Louis in 1904. He won both national and regional critical praise for his own practice in San Francisco, established in 1905. Unlike other structures at the PPIE, which were classical or Renaissance in inspiration, Mullgardt's Court of the Ages was an imaginative synthesis of styles, although it was commonly characterized as Spanish in derivation. It was more original than the similar Spanish Colonial Revival–style buildings of the Panama-California Exposition in San Diego in 1915, which were taken as a stylistic model for monumental public buildings in California.

His addition to the de Young was of reinforced concrete construction coated with stucco, with lavish use of concrete ornament on the exterior.[22] The spacious interiors were lit by natural light from above (there was no electric light in the galleries in the early years). The structure featured a courtyard with a fountain and gardens, and a high central tower that was the focus of the design. De Young told the story that when Mullgardt was given a model of the sixteenth-century doorway from the Hospice de Santa Cruz in Toledo, Spain, left over from the PPIE, he put it in the base of the tower (it could only be used in a tall structure), and the rest of the design was generated from that fragment.

Paid for by de Young, Mullgardt's addition was an immediate popular and critical success when it opened in 1921. It had an overall Spanish character, but the building's

expansion of de Young's institution, calling it "a museum where the most valuable of California relics" would be safe, since it was one of the few such collections to survive the 1906 earthquake. Knowland predicted that the new addition "will reflect not only the beauty and spirit of California in its architecture. . . . It will also stand as a reminder of the great exposition of 1915."[20] The architect charged with bringing this about was Louis Christian Mullgardt (1866–1942),[21] then at the height of his career, whose Court of the Ages at the PPIE was considered by many an architectural high point of that fair.

When he began work on the de Young, Mullgardt was admired as an unusually inventive architect, whose

M. H. de Young's daughters Kathleen, Phyllis, and Constance at the foot of the Doré vase, one of their father's first purchases for the Memorial Museum. Phyllis is the mother of trustee Nan Tucker McEvoy and the grandmother of Nion McEvoy. Photograph by Isaiah West Taber, 1894

symbolism and allegories dealt more specifically with California than the Court of the Ages had. The niches around the main doorway depicted, in figures designed by Haig Patigian, "the successive conquerors of California and the culture they brought with them." From bottom to top, these depicted Plant and Animal Life; an Aborigine with a spear and string of fish; Spanish Conquistadors and Franciscan Padres; the Anglo-Saxon Pioneer Man and Woman; and Science, Industry, and Education. Profuse architectural ornament, interspersed with allegories, was concentrated around entranceways and corners and along the tops of the walls, a composition that attempted to mimic the vegetation of the park. The height of the tower was supposed to "make it harmonize with the tall trees of its surroundings, as the lower masses of the main wings accord . . . with the dense copses of the undergrowth. It is

to be no obtrusive feature in the landscape, out of place in a park, but almost an atmospheric effect among the trees, or, to use another figure, the building is to be rather an undertone in the woodland setting."[23]

When the Mullgardt building opened, the *Chronicle* was predictably extravagant in its praise, calling it "a building of bewildering loveliness."[24] More sober but still enthusiastic appraisals were made in the architectural press,[25] including *Western Architect*, where the prominent critic Rexford Newcomb wrote:

The work of Mr. Mullgardt rings true to the highest canons of art and eloquently exemplifies those underlying fundamentals that, from the days of the Egyptians down, have been typical of architectural expression at its best.[26]

Stylistically, the Mullgardt design put the de Young

Left: M. H. de Young commissioned the expansion of the Memorial Museum from Louis Christian Mullgardt (1866–1942), whose architectural offices were in de Young's San Francisco Chronicle Building. Completed in two phases in 1919 and 1921, it had an overall Spanish character with a fountain and gardens.

Right: Mullgardt's main entrance was embellished with an allegory of the settling of California. In front was the Pool of Enchantment (1920), by sculptor Earl Cummings.

Museum on the edge of mainstream American museum architecture. It was unusual in that the exterior style was neither classical nor Renaissance in derivation, and in the contrasting simplicity of its interior spaces, which recalled contemporary exposition halls rather than grand historical rooms. Mullgardt's plan called for embellishments created by other artists. Surviving today at the de Young is the Pool of Enchantment by the sculptor Earl Cummings. Its theme is "Harmony Overcoming Discord," and it features "an American Pan—an Indian boy" who enchants "a pair of California mountain lions" by his playing.[27] In 1925 de Young added another wing, by the architects Weekes and Day.

During the long period of de Young's leadership, from 1895 to 1925, both the museum's attendance and the collection grew substantially. It had opened with 471,777 visitors, which grew to more than 500,000 in 1901, and more than 700,000 in 1915. In 1921, the year Mullgardt's addition was completed, "the museum boasted an attendance equaling New York's Metropolitan Museum and surpassing that of the Smithsonian Institution."[28] In 1924, a charter amendment passed the November city elections, which made the museum's official name the M. H. de Young Memorial Museum and set up a Board of Trustees to run it. Final approval to establish the Board of Trustees was given on 21 January 1925. M. H. de Young died on 15 February 1925.

CENTRAL EXPANSION AND REMODELING

In 1928, Herbert Fleishhacker and George T. Cameron, representing the park's commission and Board of Trustees, initiated a major expansion of the museum. The raw

The Mullgardt additions were constructed of reinforced concrete and coated in stucco. Lavish ornament was concentrated at the entrance, the corners, and the tops of walls. Considered an earthquake hazard, the deteriorating concrete ornament was stripped from the building's exterior when it was "modernized" in 1949.

The museum in 1920, with the central tower flanked by two gallery wings and the Pool of Enchantment at the entrance. Still standing at the eastern end (right) are the Fine Arts Building, the Royal Bavarian Pavilion, and the Canadian Pavilion (curator's residence), all of which were demolished in 1929. Louis Christian Mullgardt's west wing was demolished in 1964 and replaced by the Brundage Wing, later called the Asian Art Museum. The east wing and tower were eventually demolished in 2002.

concrete spaces of the Mullgardt addition, which once evoked the romance of the expositions, had come to seem merely cold as these associations were forgotten. Frederick H. Meyer, in association with Mark T. Jorgensen and Lawrence Keyser, designed a rear expansion with fifty new galleries that did not significantly alter the public appearance of Mullgardt's building.[29] This expansion, along with demolition of the 1894 Egyptian-style building and the Royal Bavarian Pavilion, provided the museum with a unified image for the first time. The new and remodeled interiors had a rational system of corridors that replaced the honeycomb pattern of galleries, and a very different and more harmonious atmosphere. A new classically proportioned central gallery called the Garden Court (usually referred to as the Hearst Court) was the focal point of the addition. The area that linked the wings of the Mullgardt addition was given "a Romanesque architectural treatment,"[30] consisting of red tiled floors with borders and steps in green marble terrazzo, cast-stone arches and doorways, and other decorative details in cast plaster.

When the renamed museum reopened under the direction of its trustees in 1931, it had an increased focus on art. Much of the deteriorated natural history collection had been destroyed or removed. Important works of art were coming to the museum, such as the collection of pre-Columbian gold objects, and two Italian Renaissance paintings, the first of many donations by Samuel H. Kress.[31] The position of director was established and filled by Lloyd La Page Rollins, who came to the de Young after studies at Harvard University and work at its Fogg Museum of Art.[32] Initially hired in 1930 as director of the de Young's sister museum, the California Palace of the Legion of Honor, Rollins was appointed to the de Young a few months later, joining the two institutions under one head. He divided the collections, with the Legion of Honor housing painting and sculpture, and the de Young having the decorative and graphic arts. Rollins installed period rooms and was responsible for international exhibitions of Russian icons and posters, Spanish textiles, Cambodian and Siamese sculpture, and the famous Group f.64 show of Bay Area photographers, including Imogen Cunningham, Edward Weston, and Ansel Adams. The *Chronicle* noted that the public would "be astonished by the almost complete metamorphosis of the institution."[33] It was said to be the best attended of any museum in the country.

In 1933, Rollins was succeeded by Walter Heil. Under Heil, who served until 1961, the de Young became exclusively an art museum. A scholar of Italian art with a doctorate from the University of Munich, Heil had served as a curator at the Detroit Institute of Arts. Among the exhibitions under his direction were a 1935 show of American art, a 1937 show of Islamic and Near Eastern art, and a popular 1938 show, *Three Centuries of European and American Domestic Silver.* Heil sought to create not a series of separate collections, but "a sequence of memorials to life as lived at various times and places,"[34] a modification of the period-room concept. This required substantial interior renovation, with the work done by federal relief program workers from SERA and the WPA.[35] When the museum reopened on 23 February 1937, the *Chronicle* called it "the most modern and complete gallery in the United States."[36]

PROPOSED WING: SANTA MARIA DE OVILA

On 21 May 1941, the San Francisco Board of Supervisors acquired a dismantled twelfth-century stone monastery from the publisher William Randolph Hearst with the intention to rebuild it as an addition to the M. H. de Young Memorial Museum. The monastery of Santa Maria de Ovila, built on the Tagus River eighty miles from Madrid, was an important example of Cistercian architecture. Having been damaged during the Spanish Civil War, then purchased by Hearst, it was brought to San Francisco in eleven ships at a cost of about $1 million. The city bought it for approximately $30,000, the cost of storage since it arrived in San Francisco. Although plans were prepared by the architect Julia Morgan for reconstructing the monastery next to the museum, to be paid for with WPA funds, the project was derailed by World War II. Most of the stones remained in a pile in Golden Gate Park, where they were visible to passers-by, until 1994 when they were sold to the Abbey of New Clairvaux, a Trappist-Cistercian community in Vina, California, north of Chico.

THE EXTERIOR REMODELING OF 1949

The ornate concrete decoration on the Mullgardt addition began to deteriorate about ten years after it was completed in 1921. Although the crumbling ornament was considered a safety hazard during earthquakes, this problem was not resolved for almost twenty years. In 1940, the Board of Trustees approved plans for exterior alterations by Arthur Brown Jr. and Frederick H. Meyer, both prominent San Francisco architects. It was not until 1949, after funding was provided by a 1948 bond issue, that the work was done.[37] The de Young was one of several American museums remodeled in the 1930s and 1940s to suit modern tastes in architecture and new ideas about museum building. The modernized de Young, however, was not an architectural success. In 1980, museum director Ian White wrote, "The architecture is disconcertingly anonymous today, obtrusive in its wooded setting."[38] Whereas Mullgardt's ornate design realized his intention of harmonizing with its park setting, ironically, the new, stripped-down design was at the same time less noticeable and more out of place.

NEW COLLECTIONS AND FACILITIES

In the 1950s, the focus of change at the de Young shifted decisively from the museum building to the collections.

This was primarily a result of the institution's burgeoning relationships with donors and collectors, resulting in significant acquisitions. The first of these were the Samuel H. Kress and Roscoe F. and Margaret H. Oakes collections, primarily of European painting. The new Kress Memorial Galleries and the Oakes Garden Court, designed by Weihe, Frick, and Kruse, former partners of Arthur Brown Jr., opened on 16 February 1955. The Kress wing was added to the rear of the 1931 expansion and designed in harmony with it, while the Oakes garden was a replica of an eighteenth-century French garden, with trellises and statuary.

The next important collection to come to the de Young was the Avery Brundage Collection of Asian art. Negotiations to acquire the Brundage Collection began in the late 1950s, leading to a successful bond election in 1960 for an annex to house it. Construction took place in 1965 under the leadership of Jack R. McGregor, an authority on eighteenth-century French furniture, who had come to the de Young from the Metropolitan Museum of Art in New York, and who succeeded Walter Heil as director in 1963.[39] The Brundage annex, designed by a respected San Francisco Modernist architect, Gardner Dailey,[40] involved replacing the west wing with a larger structure that would maintain the same appearance in front. In 1973, the city established the Asian Art Museum of San Francisco there, as a separate entity with its own administration. In 1970, the director of the Palace of the Legion of Honor, Ian McKibbin White, was made director of the de Young as well, both to oversee a major van Gogh exhibition and as a new trial effort at integrating the two museums; they officially merged as the Fine Arts Museums of San Francisco following a 1972 city charter amendment. White studied architecture and industrial design at Harvard and UCLA. He was assistant director at the Brooklyn Museum and continued to work as a designer before coming to San Francisco. White oversaw

Golden Gate Park's Beaux-Arts Music Concourse in the late 1920s,
with its pollarded plane trees, Spreckels Temple of Music (left), M. H.
de Young Memorial Museum (top), and California Academy of
Sciences (bottom).

A HISTORY OF THE DE YOUNG

The M. H. de Young Memorial Museum as it looked prior to the exterior bracing that was required following the damage caused by the 1989 Loma Prieta earthquake

major exhibitions such as *Andrew Wyeth* in 1973 and *Treasures of Tutankhamen* in 1979, the latter of which broke attendance records with 1.8 million visitors. Following a bicentennial exhibition of the American art collection of John D. Rockefeller 3rd, a substantial part of that collection was donated to the de Young in 1978, a gesture that significantly strengthened its holdings in American art. Among the notable paintings in the Rockefeller donation were Grant Wood's *Dinner for Threshers* and Winslow Homer's *The Bright Side.*

The support of Phyllis Wattis, a major San Francisco patron of cultural, educational, and scientific organizations, was instrumental in White's establishment of permanent galleries for the art of Africa, Oceania, and the Americas in 1973. The AOA galleries, as they were known, opened with the exhibition *African Textiles and the Decorative Arts.* A key bequest to that collection were mural fragments from Teotihuacán, which were stabilized in the new conservation laboratories, established in 1978–79.

In 1987, Harry S. Parker III succeeded White as director of the Fine Arts Museums. A Harvard graduate, Parker had worked at the Metropolitan Museum of Art in New York and served as director of the Dallas Museum of Art. In San Francisco, under his leadership, the two museums were redefined. All of the European art was centered at the Palace of the Legion of Honor, and the growing collections of art of Africa, Oceania, and the Americas, including the art of the United States, were assigned to the de Young.

THE EARTHQUAKE AND ITS CONSEQUENCES

The 1989 Loma Prieta earthquake, which damaged both the Legion of Honor and the de Young museum buildings, was a defining moment for the Fine Arts Museums. At the Legion the situation led to a major expansion, as well as reorganization and refurbishment of the galleries. During the years following the earthquake, Parker and the Board of Trustees explored various alternatives for the de Young: to restore or replace the museum building, or to move it out of the park altogether. When it was determined that the museum could not be repaired, they decided to demolish the existing building and build a new museum on the site. Farewell ceremonies for the old de Young were held between 30 December and 31 December 2000, with the museum open all night. The building closed permanently at 5:00 P.M., 31 December 2000. Demolition of the de Young began in March 2002 and was completed that June. The wing housing the Asian Art Museum was closed in late 2002 and was demolished in 2003.

The demolition and replacement of the old de Young serve as the capstone of Harry Parker's tenure. As director of the Dallas Museum of Art in the 1980s, Parker oversaw the building of a new museum by architect Edward Larrabee Barnes. When he was hired by the de Young, Parker had a record as a director who knew how to build a new museum, but he did not expect that he would have to do so again in San Francisco. The earthquake ensured otherwise. Thus, at the beginning of the twenty-first century, the de Young was in a similar situation to the one in which it had found itself a century earlier.

FORM FOLLOWS FRICTION:
THE STRUGGLE TO BUILD THE NEW DE YOUNG

Mitchell Schwarzer

San Francisco is a difficult city when it comes to architectural projects. Builders must confront the city's ethos of individualism, its passionate and sometimes peculiar special interests, and its habitually conflicting points of view. Such factors and many more came into play from 1989 to 2005, as the M. H. de Young Memorial Museum attempted and finally succeeded in demolishing its old building and constructing a new building in Golden Gate Park. Anyone who did not read the stream of newspaper articles, or ride the waves of seemingly endless public discussion, will find it hard to imagine the passions and frustrations that fueled the civic struggle to build the new de Young, San Francisco's oldest and largest art museum.

The decision to embark on a new museum building was not undertaken lightly. The Loma Prieta earthquake of 1989 uncovered severe seismic flaws in the old building. A comprehensive and costly retrofitting was required. Some aspects of the museum were in need of renovation. Interior spaces were cramped, poorly connected, and had only been minimally modernized with respect to fire and environmental codes. The de Young had also failed to adapt to the citizenry's changing vision for Golden Gate Park. Like most museums in that era, it needed to attract larger and more diverse audiences in order to provide public programs and exhibitions, but the fact that most people arrived by car conflicted with a growing public sentiment to banish automobiles within the park. As it stood, before the 1989 earthquake, the old building provided an

inadequate home for its art and poor access for its audience.

The sixteen years of planning and building the new de Young break down into three phases. First, from 1989 to 1996, the museum assessed the work that would be needed to bring the old complex up to date, and then came up with a plan to construct a new facility in the park along with an underground parking garage. Between 1996 and 1998 the fortunes of the museum flowed back and forth like the tides of San Francisco Bay. After the close defeat of the November 1996 bond issue, largely because of

Above and opposite: In 1994 bracing of steel I-beams was attached to the exterior of the museum, which was damaged in the 1989 Loma Prieta earthquake.

opposition to the parking garage, the de Young tried to move out of the park. In the midst of this process, however, swayed by popular sentiment, the museum went back to a version of its earlier park idea, crusaded once again for the new building and parking garage, and was once again narrowly defeated in the June 1998 election. Finally, in the fall of 1998, the Board of Trustees decided to build without public money, and undertook a fundraising campaign as well as the selection process for an architect of international stature. The struggle did not end with the selection of the Swiss architects Herzog & de Meuron in January of 1999. For several more years, vocal residents and citizen's groups waged a dogged fight against the architects' vision. It took until January 2002 for the San Francisco Board of Supervisors to approve the project. Over these years, the struggle to build the new de Young may be seen as a mirror into San Francisco's fractured vision of its urban future.

IN THE WAKE OF THE QUAKE
On 17 October 1989, at 5:04 P.M., a major earthquake, registering 7.1 on the Richter scale, struck the San Francisco Bay Area. Centered sixty miles south of the city, near Loma Prieta Mountain, the quake lasted twenty seconds. Scores of buildings and structures collapsed, including part of a major freeway, and thousands were damaged. Sixty-two people died. Unreinforced masonry bearing-wall buildings and structures built atop landfill proved to be most deadly. Estimated costs for rebuilding exceeded $7 billion.

At the museum in Golden Gate Park, the damage did not seem serious, at least initially. Because of preventive seismic measures taken shortly before the quake struck, the collections suffered only minimal harm. Thirty objects out of some 3,000 on display were damaged. These were mainly heavy stone sculptures or ceramics that tumbled. As for the buildings themselves, the main damage consisted of cracked plaster, cracked floor tiles, and grout loosened from stonework.[1]

Worse news was to follow, however. In 1993, an updated seismic assessment was released, which gave the museum its highest hazard rating. As the report stated, "the existing museum is not capable of withstanding the effects of a great earthquake, and probably not even a lesser major earthquake, without sustaining extensive structural and nonstructural damage resulting in significant falling hazards, or possible structural collapse, which would pose very high life safety hazards to occupants."[2] There was great potential for structural collapse in the four central buildings. Other parts of the complex revealed critical deficiencies. Retrofitting work was estimated to cost tens of millions of dollars, and would necessitate closing the museum for at least a year and a half. In February 1994, as a stopgap measure, an exterior skeleton of steel I-beams was attached to the perimeter of the museum. As *San Francisco Weekly* reporter Ellen McGarrahan lamented at the time, the building "looks like it has been flayed alive. Steel braces prop it up, 6,000 bolts screwed into the patchy stucco tower."[3]

Was the old complex worth rebuilding? Back in 1988, a different city study had already identified numerous problems in addition to deficiencies with regard to seismic safety. The de Young actually comprised not one building but six separate structures, constructed over many decades, dating back to 1916. Space for storage and classrooms was insufficient. People with disabilities could not easily access portions of the complex. Eighty percent of the complex lacked heating, cooling, or humidity control. Most building systems—especially fire and life safety— were out of date.[4] A subsequent internal study, completed in 1995, confirmed and detailed the widespread flaws of the facility.

Harry Parker, who had become director of the Fine Arts Museums of San Francisco in 1987, was not someone to opt for band-aid solutions. Before coming to San Francisco, Parker had built a new building for the Dallas Museum of Art, in a new downtown location. Once in San Francisco, he embarked on an ambitious campaign to modernize and energize both the de Young and its sister museum, the Palace of the Legion of Honor in Lincoln Park. Parker consolidated their operations and expanded fundraising and acquisitions. He physically reorganized the two museums, which had merged officially in 1970 but had not integrated their collections; henceforth, the Legion would showcase European art, while the de Young would be a repository for the art of the United States, the Americas, Africa, and Oceania. Parker also redefined the de Young's collecting policy by expanding into the twentieth and (eventually) the twenty-first centuries.

As a new director, Parker realized that the Fine Arts Museums' buildings were inadequate. His first large-scale building task was the renovation of the Legion. Unlike the de Young, the Palace of the Legion of Honor was a building of considerable architectural merit and historic interest; its 1924 design was based on a pavilion from the 1915 Panama-Pacific Exposition that itself had been modeled on a celebrated French neoclassical building, the Hôtel de Salm in Paris. Taking advantage of a city bond issue that passed immediately after the earthquake, the Legion was rebuilt between 1992 and 1995.

If history was preserved at the Legion's site in Lincoln Park, however, the future would take hold in Golden Gate Park. Early estimates for the seismic work needed at the de Young exceeded $60 million. Since the old museum buildings were deemed to be of no great architectural significance, and the classical Legion had been preserved, the trustees were amenable to erecting a brand new building in Golden Gate Park. In 1995, shortly before the

Legion reopened, the trustees voted to proceed with the complete demolition of the de Young buildings. A year later they decided to include an underground parking facility in the plan. The bulk of the money would be raised by a bond measure, Proposition B, authorizing $73.3 million, to be decided by voters in the November 1996 election. The amount of the bond was determined by the amount of money the museum would have had to spend on structural and seismic work if it had chosen to repair the old building. The additional costs for a new building—estimated at $44 million—and a 300-space parking garage would be raised privately.

In 1996 San Francisco voters narrowly defeated Proposition B, which would have authorized $73.3 million in city funds to rebuild the earthquake-damaged museum. A similar bond issue in 1998 also failed to gain the two-thirds majority required.

Proposition B was a general-obligation bond issue requiring the approval of two-thirds of San Francisco's voters. It lost by a hairline. The Proposition was defeated because of vociferous opposition by environmentalists, special-interest sports advocates—cyclists, skateboarders, rollerskaters—and residents from surrounding neighborhoods, such as the Inner Sunset, and especially the Haight-Ashbury. The parking garage was the lightning rod for the opposition. Even though it would be underground, beneath the museum, and its entrance would be on the perimeter of the Golden Gate Park, to many citizens the mere mention of a parking garage was a frightening reminder of past mega-projects such as the 1925 erection of the 60,000-seat Kezar Stadium atop the park's Rhododendron Dell, or the ultimately defeated freeway plans of the 1950s that would have wound a tight-fitting necklace of concrete around the park's forests, meadows, and lakes.

CAUGHT BETWEEN A GARAGE AND A GREEN PLACE

By the 1990s, the citizenry's philosophy regarding automobiles in the park could be characterized as less is more. Park advocacy groups sought to expand closures of major park roads, adding Saturday to the existing Sunday closures, and to remove on-street parking along roads within the park. They described the park as their "sanctuary" and "sylvan retreat." One letter to the editor in the *San Francisco Examiner* went so far as to compare Golden Gate Park, a manmade city park, to Yosemite National Park in the Sierra Nevada, equating them as two splendid natural environments overrun by automobiles.[5] Many park advocates had a problem with any buildings or automobiles in the park. In public meetings, a representative of the Coalition for Golden Gate Park stated that she wanted the park to be more of a park. When Supervisor Michael Yaki mentioned partially reversing

Sunday road closures near the museum, Paul Dorn, director of the San Francisco Bicycle Coalition, retorted, "It's Golden Gate Park, not Golden Gate Parking lot."[6] A representative of the California Outdoor Roller Skating Association argued that the goals of the museum visitors and recreational users were diametrically opposed, as they evidently were in the minds of those whose primary goal was a ban on automobiles in the park on weekends.

The 1990s debate recalled a much earlier battle, fought in the 1890s, one that resulted in the creation of the de Young Museum. The intention of Golden Gate Park's mid-nineteenth-century designer, William Hammond Hall, was to create a bucolic pleasure garden, whose purpose was to be a refuge from the congestion of city life. For its first superintendent, John McLaren, this purpose specifically excluded large-scale cultural buildings, but *San Francisco Chronicle* publisher Michael de Young had a different vision. Aware that gardens and parks had long blended the pastoral with the cultural, de Young sought to use the park's naturalistic scenery as backdrop for a resplendent display of world art and civilization that would draw attention to the city. In 1894 he successfully overrode McLaren's objections to using the park as the site of the Midwinter International Exposition, modeled on the

Above and opposite: Golden Gate Park was conceived as a refuge from the urban environment. Whether or not it should include cultural buildings has been a matter of debate since its inception in the nineteenth century.

Chicago World's Columbian Exposition of 1893, on the grounds that all of the fair buildings would be temporary. Once the fair closed, however, de Young successfully petitioned the Park Commissioners to keep the Egyptian-style Fine Arts Building, the one structure that had been intentionally built to standards of durable construction, as a permanent museum in the park. McLaren dramatized his own position by dynamiting other buildings the moment the fair ended, including the popular Bonet Electrical Tower,

a whimsical steel structure that stood 266 feet in height.

Where parks are concerned, one person's paradise can be another person's poison. Park designers of the nineteenth century, including Hall and McLaren, had been inspired by English picturesque gardens, with their serpentine meadows and lakes framed by thick walls of forest. They saw their task as remaking the natural environment, moving earth, creating lakes, and importing a multitude of plants, primarily exotic species. The vulnerability of his new plantings had been McLaren's practical reason for fearing the construction and foot traffic that a world's fair would impose on his park. With quite a different set of values, today's native-plant enthusiasts scorn the park's non-native species; theirs is a vision of a park in its pre-1850s condition, sand dunes punctuated by scrub-coastal vegetation, and hardly a tall tree in sight.

Over the decades, horticulturalists and activists of all stripes have routinely tried to limit other uses of Golden Gate Park, whether recreational or cultural. Yet in the course of its almost 150-year history, the park has steadily expanded its range of attractions. Its roughly one thousand acres accommodate baseball diamonds and a polo field, two ornamental windmills, public sculpture, an arboretum, a Japanese Tea Garden, a buffalo paddock, and a Music Concourse, as well as two major museums; an art museum, the de Young, and a museum of natural history, the California Academy of Sciences. An extensive system of roads provides parking places for local and suburban visitors who use the park, as well as some commuters who then take nearby transit to their workplaces. High-speed roadways, such as Park Presidio Boulevard, By-Pass Drive, and Cross-Over Drive, slice through the heart of the park, providing vital connections between adjacent neighborhoods.

In reality, the greenish piece of land named Golden Gate Park has many uses and it sparks even more ideas on what its uses should and should not be. Ironically, many of the opponents of the new de Young museum parking garage were not advocates of horticulture, or playing fields, or public art. They were skaters and cyclists seeking open space threaded by hard surfaces upon which they could glide. The section of the park they wanted for themselves was near the museums, the very roads and parking lots that had been put in to accommodate visitors to the museums and other cultural attractions. Their ideal of a largely

automobile-free park would not have been possible without the earlier creation of asphalt and concrete roads for automobiles.

These same roads were used by people coming to the de Young. Like all major museums in the 1990s, the de Young needed to keep increasing the number of its visitors in order to survive financially and thrive culturally. Traditionally, almost 75 percent of the de Young's audience came not from the city of San Francisco but from the Bay

The Japanese Tea Garden, dating from the 1894 California International Midwinter Exposition, is one of the many distinctive areas within Golden Gate Park.

Area, Northern California, and beyond. What could the museum do to improve access for all visitors? Opponents of the parking garage argued for alternative transportation to the museum, such as shuttle buses that would connect to nearby light-rail lines or temporary satellite parking lots. Shuttles had worked well for popular temporary exhibits, where visitors planned their trip to the museum in advance. The museum ran a shuttle for the blockbuster Monet exhibition in 1995 and the Fabergé and Peru shows in 1996, but canceled them afterward because of low usage. Apparently, the public would not rely on the shuttles for impromptu visits. Would tourists and residents of other Bay Area cities find their way to a Muni stop, take the Muni, and then transfer to a shuttle bus? The reality was that in car-conscious California, between 50 and 70 percent of visitors customarily came to the museum by automobile.

In June 1997, with the fate of the new building in limbo, the news got worse. The museum was informed that it could no longer receive federal indemnification for traveling art exhibits. Even with the bracing, the old buildings were too dangerous. The de Young now stood to lose millions of dollars annually. Some big-budget shows could go to the much smaller Legion, but many would bypass the Bay Area entirely. By September 1997, Parker began to worry openly about the increasingly bleak attendance figures. He was well aware that, because of the Sunday ban on cars, the de Young was one of the few American museums to have lower attendance on Sunday than Saturday. As he put it, the museum: "is in a vicious negative circle, with trends toward fewer visitors and lower revenues. We have to break this vicious circle, and soon, or we risk the closure of the de Young."[7]

Averaged over a ten-year period in the 1980s, approximately 650,000 people a year visited the museum. In the 1990s, attendance had rebounded from the 400,000 who visited the museum in 1990, the year after the quake, to 715,000 by 1995. It fell back to 638,000 by 1996, however, and would soon plunge to just over 300,000 in 1998. Without traveling shows, the museum would be stuck at this low level for the foreseeable future.

With these concerns in mind, the museum considered the idea of leaving the park for downtown San Francisco. In recent years, major art museums in Seattle and Denver, as well as in Dallas, had done just that. To its advocates, a downtown building would have the advantage of connecting the museum to a host of related institutions and entertainments—galleries, movie theaters, restaurants, stores, hotels. David Bonetti, the *San Francisco Examiner* art critic, argued that museums were better off downtown. As he saw it, keeping the de Young in the park would amount to preserving it in its essentially nineteenth-century context, as a retreat from urban life modeled on the aristocratic palace. He observed that a downtown de Young could jump over the twentieth century and land smack in the twenty-first. It could "be at the center of action because it is potentially the center of action."[8]

In 1997, the museum-commissioned Sedway Report predicted a 75 percent increase in attendance if the de Young moved downtown versus a 10 percent increase if it stayed in the park—757,000 versus 475,000.[9] The preferred site was at the eastern edge of the Financial District, adjacent to Embarcadero Center, where an ambitious commercial conversion of the historic Ferry Building was underway; a second choice was Pier 27-29. Both sites had better public transit access than the park, to multiple Muni lines and BART, and both could accommodate a parking garage. On the rapidly developing Embarcadero, the de Young might well enjoy a synergy with other urban activities, such as those that had energized the San Francisco Museum of Modern Art after it moved in 1995 into a new facility in the burgeoning SOMA district, on

Third Street across from Yerba Buena Gardens. It did not take long for the de Young officials to see the wisdom of a downtown move, and in the fall of 1997 the trustees voted to pursue a move out of the park. As Dede Wilsey, president of the Fine Arts Museums Board of Trustees, stated, "A world-class museum has to be accessible to all people."[10]

The idea of a downtown de Young died a swift death. Almost from the start worries were raised about traffic congestion and toxic materials in the landfill of the Mid-Embarcadero site. The biggest stumbling block, though, was the museum's desertion of Golden Gate Park.

New citizens groups sprang up, such as the Coalition to Keep the de Young in the Park. Rather than being concerned with increased visitor loads or the parking-garage controversy, these citizens argued for the importance of the park site to the museum's civic mission. One person at a public meeting lamented that moving the museum out of the park would be like closing a factory in a small town. Another compared moving the museum to moving the trees or Stow Lake. A letter to the editor of the *Chronicle* stated that "the de Young's removal is as if a Botticelli was stolen from a Renaissance exhibit."[11] To these San Franciscans, the de Young was by no means a hindrance to park enjoyment. It was the park's crown jewel. Some people feared that if the de Young moved other cultural treasures would leave as well, especially the California Academy of Sciences, which, for similar access reasons, was also contemplating a move at the time. As a resident from the Inner Sunset said in response to new of the de Young's planned move, "It's a domino effect here. . . . We're losing our major educational anchor of Golden Gate Park."[12]

As sites for a new de Young, downtown and the park each presented advantages and disadvantages. A downtown location promised the benefits of situating the museum within the nexus of everyday life, commerce, and popular culture. By contrast, the park was a wonderfully bucolic and escapist setting in which to contemplate art. A downtown location promised to attract new visitors. Some San Franciscans saw no need to attract more visitors, however, reasoning that keeping the museum in the park would keep it focused on its core constituency, city residents, which was preferable to turning it into a popular tourist attraction. A downtown location, on the other hand, promised to diversify the museum's audience. Yet the decision to leave the park was seen by some San Franciscans as elitist. According to *San Francisco Bay Guardian* reporter Daniel Zoll, "many park advocates and de Young supporters say the decision on the future of the museum is too important to be left to an unelected board of wealthy trustees, many of whom do not even live in the city."[13] No matter what it tried to do or where it tried to do it, the de Young was not going to satisfy everyone.

A particularly interesting argument concerned children. Groups such as the Coleman Advocates for Children and Youth preferred the park location because it provided children with access to other recreational options nearby: grassy fields, playgrounds, the Carousel. As a neighbor wrote, "it's more than just a trip to a museum. It's a day in the park with art on the menu for kids used to sidewalks and concrete. It's a chance to make the connection between the beauty of the setting and the attempts to capture beauty through art."[14] Only months after the defeat of the bond issue to put a concrete parking garage under the park, the sculptor Ruth Asawa stated her opposition to the downtown move: "We have just voted to move our animals from concrete to grass," referring to the recently unveiled new design for the San Francisco Zoo, "and now we're proposing to move our children from grass to concrete."[15]

Public sentiment carried the day. A poll of city residents conducted by David Binder in December 1997 found that almost 80 percent of the respondents preferred that the museum stay in the park. Not long afterward, in January

"*PAVE PARADISE,*

GOLDEN GATE PARK NURSERY 1920

PUT UP A PARKING LOT"

COMMUTER PARKING LOT TODAY

THE PARK IS UNDER ATTACK

ALLIANCE FOR GOLDEN GATE PARK

1998, largely because of this poll and others like it, the museum board voted to remain at the historic site. A little more than a year after the first failed bond issue, the de Young was back where it started.

In a fateful move, the museum, assisted by political consultants John Whitehurst and Elizabeth Colton, soon went back to the voters for bond funding to stay in the park. This time, however, the June 1998 ballot contained another measure. Proposition J authorized the building of a privately funded 800-space parking garage under the Music Concourse (to be shared by the de Young, the California Academy of Sciences, and other park users). It was sponsored and supported by citizens' groups

clamoring for the museums to stay in the park, and passed by the majority vote required. A new city commission was created, the Concourse Authority, to oversee the garage project as well as study other transit improvements in the museum vicinity and throughout the park.

The other measure, Proposition A, earmarked $89.9 million to assist in the construction a new building. Once again, it was defeated, narrowly missing the mandated two-thirds mark. In the timing of the vote, the de Young had suffered another round of bad luck. As Jim Chappell, director of San Francisco Planning and Urban Research, a public-policy think tank, explained: "A month or so before the election the Board of Supervisors passed a one-year

Anti-car and pro-sports activists waged a high-profile, but ultimately unsuccessful, campaign against rebuilding the de Young on its original site.

exception that would allow the owners of rental property to pass property tax increases onto their tenants. With tenants groups mobilized, any bond measures that could impact property taxes, like Proposition A, were doomed."[16] Another bond issue was in the works that year, the $500 million decision on whether to rebuild Laguna Honda Hospital, the city's public nursing home. In a devastating campaign, opponents of the museum bond measure posed the question to the voters as a choice between public money going for "old people" or "old paintings."

TOWERING AMBITIONS

In the summer of 1998, the museum was trapped in the stuff of bad dreams. Any idea they proposed seemed to spawn new citizens' groups and produce inflammatory newspaper headlines. The most vocal (and hence effective) of these opponents were indifferent to the goal of creating a world-class museum. They were caught up in their own interests and how these would be affected by changes in the park and at the museum. To some the park was a natural wilderness, to others a playground for acting wild; to some it was a setting for a multidimensional family outing, to others for an experience in art. The bottom line was clear. The majority of San Franciscans favored building a new museum in the park, but were uncertain as to how to go about it. Harry Parker worried that the museum had fallen into a quagmire: "We spent a great deal of time trying to satisfy the city's different constituencies. But each time we met the conditions of one group, some other group rose up with new demands."[17]

View from the entrance of the old de Young, with the Pool of Enchantment in the foreground, the Music Concourse in the middle ground, and the California Academy of Sciences beyond. The sculptures from the Pool of Enchantment and the palm trees have been repositioned at the new museum.

Shortly after the election, Dede Wilsey told a disheartened Parker and other staff members that all was not lost. As Parker recalls: "TV cameras came to take pictures of us sweeping the floor at the campaign offices. We were really depressed, but Dede got in front of the cameras and said, 'Well we've tried these bond issues, so now we're going to do it privately.' I watched her and thought, 'Oh my God, how can she say this?' It was a very spirited, spunky thing to do."[18] In the coming months, Wilsey turned the sights of the museum toward the future. In October 1998, under her leadership, the de Young trustees decided to forgo yet a third ballot bond measure and instead raise the entire $165 million for a new building and parking garage. (This figure was eventually exceeded.) With this bold action, the debate shifted from where and whether the museum would be

rebuilt to how it would be rebuilt. The time had come to search for an architect.

In the fall of 1998 the museum put out a call to architects worldwide. More than fifty firms expressed interest, site visits were held, and ultimately twenty-five firms sent in complete submissions. A technical review panel, composed primarily of outside professionals, narrowed the list to six firms of international standing. In January 1999, the selection committee, made up of donors and museum trustees, chose the Swiss firm of Herzog & de Meuron, in part because of their willingness to engage in an extended (and, in San Francisco, necessarily public) process of architectural design. More importantly, however, Herzog & de Meuron were selected because their prior work demonstrated a drive to explore new building solutions

for every client. As Deborah Frieden, the new de Young's project director, put it: "The museum wanted an architectural statement that would be unique to its vision, its collections, and its site in Golden Gate Park."[19]

Each of Herzog & de Meuron's prior buildings, most of which are in Western Europe, are known for strikingly different facade treatments—the use of uncommon materials, textures, patterns, and even rows of words. The firm would go on to win the Pritzker Prize—architecture's equivalent of the Nobel Prize—in 2001. Of the previous winners since the Prize was started in 1979, only Philip Johnson and Fumihiko Maki had built in San Francisco.

Herzog & de Meuron's initial concept for the new de Young was unveiled in June 1999. It consisted of three parallel bars that extended like fingers into the verdant park landscape. At first, the design was praised for its restraint and elegance, its nonhierarchical gallery spaces, and its subtle reading of the park context, all crucial criteria in aesthetically cautious and politically left-leaning San Francisco. Nicolai Ouroussoff, then architecture critic of the *Los Angeles Times*, applauded the "varying degrees of transparency, dissolving boundaries between inside and out and offering a variety of unexpected contexts to the weary museum-goer."[20] He also understood the architects' intention behind the monolithic roof, and how its low horizontal form would go a long way to unifying the building's interior spaces and anchoring it firmly within the expanse of Golden Gate Park.

Quite soon, however, the Herzog & de Meuron concept provoked reactions of a more disparaging kind. Frieden acknowledged that "the unveiling of the new design did not go as planned. Somehow, the building's shape, skin, and tower each became a point of contention in the newspapers. The first photographs did not help either."[21] Indeed, the *San Francisco Chronicle's* front-page article "First Look: New de Young," appearing on June 11, 1999, was a public-relations disaster. It featured two images. On the bottom was a photograph of the old de Young, centered on its tower and shot from a distance. In a small black-and-white image, it was impossible to discern either the barren stucco walls or seismic braces; the old building did not look as scarred in the photograph as in reality. A cyclist, alluding perhaps to the ongoing controversies over athletics versus art, occupied the foreground. On top, a computer rendering showed the new conceptual design. Again no details could be seen. The lack of visual texture in the black-and-white photograph produced an impression of a long, blank box, with an unflattering industrial look. And in this photo the new tower burst skyward to the very top of the frame (conceivably extending even higher). The

The architects' first published rendering of the proposed design, which appeared on 11 June 1999 in the *San Francisco Chronicle*, provoked intense criticism. The gray exterior was interpreted as glass and steel. In fact, the materials had not yet been chosen.

accompanying article stated that the new museum would have twice as much space and a taller, distinctive tower.

The *San Francisco Examiner's* image of the same rendering, published the same day, showed that the tower would indeed end. Nevertheless, a couple of days later, an *Examiner* editorial noted that a controversy over the tower was brewing and that, in the sketches, the new building resembled a huge shed. The editors admitted to the aesthetic conservatism of this socially liberal city, and encouraged San Franciscans to keep an open mind.

How likely would that be? On June 15, *Chronicle* columnist Jon Carroll compared the new design to an internet startup company, writing, "you look at the sketch, and you think, Sybase."[22] In the heat of the dot-com boom, San Franciscans did not need to hear that their great art museum would look like a tilt-up alongside Highway 101. A week or so later, another *Chronicle* columnist, Scott Ostler, was even less forgiving, commenting, "it looks like a Howard Johnson's of the future."[23] In the following months and years, metaphors from all points on the aesthetic compass abounded. The design reminded one San Franciscan of an aircraft carrier, beached in the middle of the park. Others called it "ugly," "sterile," and "atrocious." Another battle of words, echoing the debate over having buildings in the park at all, raged on over the aesthetics and cultural symbolism of the new design.

As time went on, much of the resistance to the design focused on its rectilinear composition, with the assumption that horizontality was inappropriate to the park setting, and on its proposed cladding materials. Arguments were made against glass, which had never been proposed, and against the final copper solution, as being "unnatural" in the park—even though copper is a natural material that would turn green over time and blend in with the surrounding forest. Once again, the definition of the context was as wide as the horizon of the nearby Pacific Ocean. Some opponents felt that the contemporary design conflicted with tradition, represented by the Beaux-Arts plan of the adjacent Music Concourse and bandstand. Theirs was just one reading of history, for, when it was built in 1900, some citizens had

argued that this classical set piece itself conflicted with the park's picturesque character.

Other arguments were not specific. A 2001 resolution of the Glen Park neighborhood association argued for "a design for human interaction rather than a new commercial-like building . . . a facade that will touch the human heart, rather than make a hi-tech statement." Some San Franciscans lobbied to keep the old museum buildings, with their ornament and Mediterranean stylistic touches, although they were not recognized as architecturally significant by municipal, state, or national preservationists. Decades earlier, in 1949, almost all of the museum's decorative Spanish Colonial Revival ornament had been removed. This did not keep some individuals from celebrating the old edifice. Ken Alexander, in an op-ed piece in the *San Francisco Examiner*, stated that the recently installed steel braces on the old museum's exterior serve the same purpose as the flying buttresses of Nôtre Dame in Paris, concluding: "Do you suppose Parisians would stand still for leveling Nôtre Dame and replacing it with an ecclesiastical Costco?"[24] The recent seismic bracing, understood by its structural engineer, Richard Niewiarowski, as a temporary measure to prevent catastrophic collapse, had attained, at least for this critic, historical and aesthetic value.

The architects' design was especially castigated for its tower. Certain people worried that the tower might be seen from afar, forgetting that standing high and tall above the mass of a building has defined the meaning of towers for millennia. Another citizens' group, the People for a New de Young Museum, was formed to fight against the new design and tower. Their literature described the asymmetrical, twisting tower as a fourteen-story high-rise, and emphasized its ninety-foot width. At the same time, their spokesman, Joe Fusco, likened the overall building to a cheesy motel in Vegas.[25] The new de Young could be all

bad things at once, at least to this opponent—a lofty office building and a lowly motel.

Single-issue advocates like the Alliance for Golden Gate Park opposed the tower because it might draw more vehicular traffic, attracting tourists interested in a free view of the park.[26] At a hearing at the San Francisco Planning Commission in August of 2000, their representative, Philip Carleton, said: "We go to the park to see nature, not to see monstrous human structures." Once again, as was so often the case in the struggle for the new de Young, the collective pronoun was used to characterize the sentiments of an individual. At such meetings, citizens threw out aesthetic or historical pronouncements as if they were self-evident and shared by everyone. Such was never the case. At the same Planning Commission meeting, Jim Chappell spoke out in favor of the new design, comparing it to a cathedral in a European city. As he later stated, "It is appropriate for the de Young to have a spire, a marker seen from afar, just as cathedrals did."[27]

The design controversy pitted certain types of San Franciscans against other types. Supporters of the Herzog & de Meuron building tended to be experts, museum curators, architects, artists, and academics. (A few local architects opposed the new design on the basis of its presumed radicalism as well as their resentment at the nonlocal choice.) Opponents tended to be nonspecialists devoting their free time to a cause in which they fervently believed. While adopting names that signaled large followings—"citizens for blank"—these groups were usually composed of small numbers of highly active participants. The larger citizenry occasionally weighed in, pro and con. By and large, however, the public debate was dominated by those most committed.

The architects' visual imagery did not help their case. It certainly did not speak to the public. Their renderings (in drawings or models) and working process thus inadvertently deepened the divide between the two groups—those in favor of challenging architecture and those committed to the tried and true. As Harrison Fraker, Dean of the School of Environmental Design at U.C. Berkeley, explained their imagery: "Herzog & de Meuron usually start with a simple and unimaginative diagram and then start working on it with materials and light."[28] While most architects and artists could readily envision the future building implicit within this process, since they themselves worked similarly, more literally sighted citizens' groups saw only what was presented at each stage. Eager to see finished products before they had been decided upon, they pounced on each of the architects' iterative moves. Once the architects were in the media spotlight, taking risks became hazardous.

As the park and parking garage controversy illustrated all too well, the public process that was supposed to make things happen more effectively in San Francisco could result in their not happening at all. "We've taken a lot of heat on the exterior," Parker stated in September 1999, adding that his Swiss architects were not used to "going through the public gauntlet the way San Francisco cooks it up."[29] In an op-ed piece a month later, Parker admitted that the museum board and staff always realized there would be fervent public discussion over a new design, and that the design was always intended to start from and evolve within such a process.[30] Indeed, the museum had been running extensive public meetings since 1994, inviting San Franciscans to contribute their ideas to the shaping of the new de Young. According to Pam McDonald, the museum's Director of Audience Development and Civic Affairs, two of the ideas central to Herzog & de Meuron's plan—retaining the tower as the iconic image of the museum and enhancing the relation to the park—emerged during this public process, which involved 115 meeetings.[31] Nor did the museum conduct public meetings in isolation. The city's

Recreation and Park Commission, its Planning Commission, and its Board of Supervisors ran extensive public hearings.

Between the spring of 1999, when the initial concept was unveiled, and January 2002, when a decision was made on whether the design met city requirements, it was unclear in which direction San Francisco would lean. For more than twenty years, the City Planning Department had been favoring postmodern architectural ideas based on a nostalgic vision of "historic San Francisco," spelled out in various design guidelines. Modern and contemporary architectural projects were routinely rejected. On the world scene, the city acquired a reputation as a place that was self-obsessed, withered into conformity, repeating its past histories even if mediocre. The undeniably sprawling public process was largely to blame. True, it involved citizens in the step-by-step conception of architecture, but it also involved them in an ongoing criticism that often proved deadly to that process of creation.[32]

By the turn of the twenty-first century, architectural sentiment in San Francisco had begun to look to the future. In the case of the de Young, the public process contributed to the decision to shorten the tower by sixteen feet. It encouraged the retention of particular features from the old de Young—the sphinxes, the Pool of Enchantment, the original palm trees—and their incorporation in the new design. And a lawsuit filed by the People for a New de Young Museum group delayed the approval of the Environmental Impact Report, requiring it to go before the San Francisco Board of Supervisors. The museum had prepared its case to the board meticulously, however. Staff such as Frieden and Carolyn McMillan had garnered critical supporters and effectively demonstrated that opponents of the new design had negligible backing. In January 2002, San Francisco's Board of Supervisors gave its blessing to the project, and demolition of the old buildings

began in the spring of the same year. The new building was completed in the spring of 2005.

It had taken two years, from 1998 to 2000, to form the Concourse Authority charged with building the parking garage. After a Superior Court decision in June 2004 ruled against a lawsuit by a single individual challenging the legality of using parking revenue to pay for the 400-space de Young garage, located underneath the forecourt and roads in front of the museum, its construction went forward.

TOWARD A NEW PLANNING

Planning and building the new de Young might come to be regarded as a turning point in San Francisco's urban design culture. Perhaps more than any other place in the country, the Bay Area has pioneered a new politics of citizen participation, which has led architecture out of closed offices and private boardrooms into the open, glaring, and

inchoate light of democracy. The result has been the shaping of a building not just by the wealthy and powerful, as has so often been the case in history. The de Young debate involved all manner of citizens representing all types of viewpoints. The fact that this large and diverse body politic did not derail the creation of an excellent building is a testament to those San Franciscans who believed all along in the importance of a world-class museum and worked doggedly to achieve it.

San Francisco's planning process has begun to transcend the longstanding conflict between citizen and expert. In the postwar era, powerful figures such as Justin Herman, head of the Redevelopment Agency, were able to implement sweeping plans crafted by experts in the architectural, housing, and transportation fields. Across the nation, total city redesign was the rule of the day. Beginning in the 1960s, when citizen's groups began effectively to opppose freeway and urban renewal plans,

The "topping-off" ceremony at the new de Young on 18 October 2003. A tradition originating in Scandinavia around A.D. 700, the "topping off" of a new structure with a tree assured that the building and its occupants would have good luck.

the pendulum began to swing. In San Francisco, by the 1980s, it had swung almost 180 degrees. Neighborhood change, new architecture, chain stores, and heightened urbanity became evil concepts to many San Franciscans. In the nation's counterculture capital, citizen chemists brewed a powerful mix of activism and nimbyism. Individuals and small (neighborhood or special-interest) groups could now derail even the largest projects.

By the early years of the new millennium, however, the political climate began to turn once more, away from citizen deadlock, yet not back to autocratic rule. The internal planning process for the museum included extensive input from citizens. Just as importantly, however, never before in San Francisco had so many experts— artists, architects, and academics—devoted their time to a building project. This was not a struggle between good guys and bad guys—neighborhoods and downtown, residents and tourists, or ordinary people and elites. It was

a struggle over how San Francisco's public institutions would adjust to changing times. Some of those changes undoubtedly originated with the museum and its desire for an inspiring new building along with improved parking access. Equally, many of the changes came from disparate points on the compass of the citizenry. Golden Gate Park had long been evolving from a courtly pleasure garden to a contentious public forum. The nerves touched by the museum's building ideas would likely have been touched by any plan that affected it. The collision of cultures that took place over these sixteen years was a historically inevitable stage in San Francisco's cultural development.

Hopefully the long-term benefit gained through the emotional and circuitous process of building the de Young might be a more sophisticated hybrid form of citizen-expert collaboration, aware of its own complexity. In the end, the verve and distinctiveness of the new museum speaks most eloquently to this prospect.

At eleven o'clock one hot July night in 1998, Fine Arts Museums director Harry Parker and the president of his Board of Trustees, Dede Wilsey, were picking their way through the wasteland of the Basel train yards, as the lights of town twinkled unreassuringly in the distance. They were on a quest known to many devotees of contemporary architecture: trying to find the Signal Box. A switching station designed for the Swiss national railroad by the Basel architects Herzog & de Meuron, the Signal Box caused a sensation in the architecture world when the building was completed in 1994. In photographs, it is an object of commanding presence: a shimmering windowless volume, entirely covered by twisting strips of copper. But like many iconic photographs, images of the Signal Box offer few clues as to where the building is and what surrounds it. In this case its context, the vast stretches of the Basel train yards, is large and chaotic, within which the Signal Box is small and hard to find.

Like other architecture pilgrims before them, Wilsey and Parker had set out confidently from their hotel in the center of Basel, having uttered the words "architect" and "train station" to a willing taxi driver. An hour later, they were wandering among railroad tracks and outbuildings at what felt like the end of the world. "The taxi wouldn't go any farther," Parker recollected with amusement. "So we finally had to get out and walk. It was dark and Dede was wearing her Chanel slingbacks. But that did not stop her from clambering over the tracks. The night shift was

starting, and some workmen appeared and showed us the building. They could not have been more polite, but we must have looked like creatures from outer space."

Parker and Wilsey had come to Basel not to see the work of Herzog & de Meuron but to inspect a new private museum by the Italian architect Renzo Piano, the Beyeler Foundation. A low-slung glass and stone pavilion, nestled alongside open fields on the outskirts of town, the Beyeler had opened to critical acclaim the previous year. Piano is a highly respected figure in museum design. As a young architect, he and his partner Richard Rogers electrified the

The Basel train yard, with the SSB Signal Box Auf dem Wolf (1994) in the distance

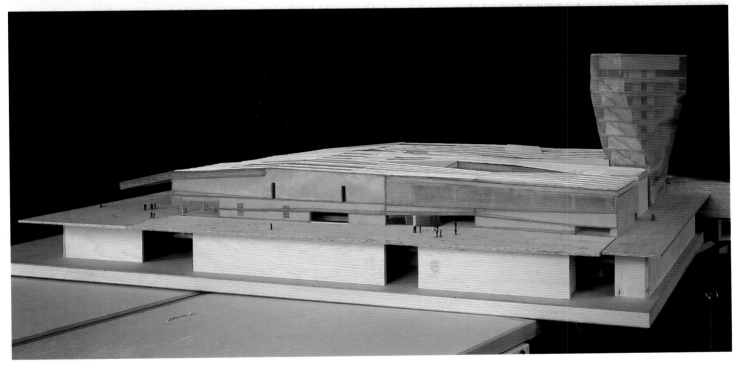

Drawing and model of the new de Young

art world with their 1977 Centre Pompidou in Paris, with its provocative exposed ductwork, vibrant colors, and extravagantly scaled public spaces. In 1987 Piano produced an understated gallery for the Menil Collection in Houston that is considered a masterpiece of twentieth-century architecture. It was followed by the Brancusi Studio in Paris and the Cy Twombly Gallery in Houston, where the distinctive feature is natural overhead light, with floating ceilings that hide the mechanical components. Piano's 1997

Beyeler museum, though not situated in a city park like the de Young, occupies a parklike setting between protected agricultural land and quiet suburbs. The Menil is in a residential neighborhood of Houston. Both the Menil and the Beyeler are notably sensitive to their natural and social environments, and for this reason alone, Piano was an obvious candidate to design a museum in Golden Gate Park, a 1,000-acre Olmsted-inspired park in a primarily residential part of San Francisco.

The copper-clad Signal Box (1994), Basel

In the summer of 1998, Parker and Wilsey, who were eager to begin the search for an architect for the de Young, decided to make a two-day trip to Switzerland to see Piano's new museum in the Basel suburb of Riehen. They had an appointment with the client, the local art dealer and collector Ernst Beyeler, but intended to tour the museum as ordinary visitors. "Who should we run into but Renzo Piano," Wilsey recounted. "He just happened to be there that day. We had a pleasant chat as we walked through the galleries, but we were not convinced that he would be right for us." Parker and Wilsey's visit to Basel appeared to have been fruitless.

Or so it seemed that evening, as they dined on the terrace of the Three Kings Hotel. When Wilsey took a phone call from her son in California, Parker picked up his copy of Victoria Newhouse's just-published book on museum architecture. A photograph of a railroad building by Herzog & de Meuron caught his eye.[1] The hotel was not far from the Basel train station. "By the time we finished dinner," Parker remembered, "a visit to the railyard seemed like an excellent idea."

The next morning, Parker looked up Herzog & de Meuron in the phone book at the hotel. "Harry Gugger, who took our call, regretted that a meeting was not possible. Then I had an idea. I said we had come from California to see Renzo Piano's museum. With the mention of the Beyeler, a free half hour suddenly appeared in the architects' schedule. Jacques's first question after we shook hands was: 'And what did you think of the Beyeler?'"[2]

Of that first meeting with Jacques Herzog and Pierre de Meuron, Wilsey said, "They were not aggressive salesmen, they were reserved." She was charmed by their office, a nineteenth-century villa just off the river in the old part of Basel. "The rooms had moldings and were painted in warm colors," she remembered. "I knew their work was contemporary, but I thought it was a good sign that they worked in a building from the past." Wilsey was sufficiently impressed that when Jacques Herzog and Pierre de Meuron came to the Napa Valley a few months later to discuss the Kramlich residence, she invited them to her home in nearby Rutherford to give a slide presentation to her selection committee. The same weekend, she took the committee to see the architects' only American building, Dominus Winery, which was just down the road. "We had personal contact with Herzog & de Meuron from early on," Parker said. "This was not true of any other architects in the competition, whom we got to know later. Who knows what would have happened if I hadn't made that phone call from the hotel, if they hadn't had a half hour to see us before our flight back to San Francisco?"

Parker and Wilsey's adventures in search of an architect had begun on Election Day, 2 June 1998, when they awaited the results of a second city bond issue to rebuild the earthquake-damaged de Young museum. Once again, the San Francisco voters withheld the two-thirds majority required. The measure, Proposition A, failed narrowly, by 1.7 percent. The next morning, Wilsey told Parker: "We will raise the money ourselves." Looking back to that

The Herzog & de Meuron office, Basel

moment, she said, "Suddenly, we could think about what we really wanted."

San Francisco has a reputation for being conservative in its architecture. It is a commonplace that the city's fabled beauty owes less to its buildings than to its natural setting, with its hills, Mediterranean light, and views of the bay. The Northern California city is compared unfavorably to Los Angeles, whose rambunctious architecture scene made it a mecca for cultural tourists from the 1970s onward.[3] San Francisco's civic architecture appeared especially lackluster during the years when Los Angeles was emerging as an international leader. During the 1990s boom, with its vogue of the signature cultural building, it was embarrassing to some San Franciscans that neither the Rotterdam-based Rem Koolhaas nor Frank Gehry, a Californian, lauded throughout the world for his startling and expressive designs, had received a commission in their city. In 1998, the year in which Parker and Wilsey met with Herzog & de Meuron in Basel, the most touted architect in San Francisco was Robert A. M. Stern, who occupied the opposite end of the stylistic spectrum from Gehry and the L.A. School. An East Coast architect known for his reinterpretations of historical styles, Stern was in charge of the headquarters for Gap Inc. and a residence for art dealer John Berggruen. In the civic realm, the comparisons were pointed. While Los Angeles was courting risk and glory with Frank Gehry designing the Disney Concert Hall, and Seattle had commissioned Rem Koolhaas for its new Central Library, San Francisco had erected two cultural buildings that were far less adventurous: the San Francisco Museum of Modern Art by the Lugano-based architect Mario Botta and the San Francisco Main Public Library by James Freed of Pei Cobb Freed. There were exceptions, especially outside the city center. But for its cultural institutions, San Francisco had built nothing by 1998 that met that decade's definition of exciting architecture. One

asked what the city had to show for the economic boom of the 1990s.

Enter the de Young museum, with its mandate to build. It had an important choice to make vis-à-vis the state of public architecture. There was, on the one hand, a groundswell of opinion that San Francisco was long overdue to have a cutting-edge museum building. On the other hand, there was a mood of anticipatory nostalgia for the art museum in the park, a fixture of city life since 1894, which was about to be demolished. Beloved by many, the old, familiar de Young was in a traditional architectural style, Spanish Colonial Revival, that some believed was still eminently fitting for California and the park. When the fate of the museum was being debated immediately after the 1989 earthquake, postmodern historicism did not have the low repute that it would later earn. At that moment, a historicist exercise by Stern, Michael Graves, or Philip Johnson might well have been a candidate to replace the old de Young. By the time the museum abandoned hope of public funding in 1998, however, nearly ten years had passed. Historicism was no longer the favored solution to the dilemma of whether to please traditionalists or those impatient to have an example of the new architecture in San Francisco.

SELECTING AN ARCHITECT

The shock of electoral defeat changed the museum's position in this longstanding discussion. Now it would be rebuilding the de Young on its own. This was no small order, given the need for immediate action. The damaged museum, although officially unsafe, was still in daily use. The campaign to raise private money, initially set at $89 million, had to capitalize on the sense of urgency over earthquake danger stirred up by the bond issue. Being financially independent from the city had a galvanizing effect on Wilsey and her board.

Top, left to right: Jacques Herzog, Pierre de Meuron,
Harry Gugger, Christine Binswanger

Above: Model of the de Young and samples of copper
panels in Herzog & de Meuron's Basel office

"Oddly, we felt excited," Wilsey said. "After four years of putting all of our efforts into winning at the voting booth, it was liberating to know that we could just go forward and build the museum that we wanted." Looking back in 2005, Parker called the defeat of the bond issue, "the best thing that ever happened to us. It freed us in our thinking about the architecture. With private funding, we could be more adventurous. We could take some risks."

Their umbrella organization, the Fine Arts Museums of San Francisco, had previously worked with architect Edward Larrabee Barnes. Soon after the 1989 Loma Prieta earthquake, in 1991, Barnes's office began the seismic retrofit and underground expansion of the de Young's sister museum, the Legion of Honor, where the European collections are housed. Built in 1924, the Legion was a replica of a historic building from the eighteenth century, the Hôtel de Salm in Paris, much admired by Thomas Jefferson. Its renovation by Barnes, as would be expected, was a decorous historicist exercise. At the same time, Barnes had also sketched out a rudimentary master plan for the part of Golden Gate Park occupied by the de Young museum. By 1998, however, Barnes's office had closed, and Wilsey and her selection committee were in a position to start afresh with a new architect.

"Even though the museum was being built with private money, we thought it was important to have a competition," said Wilsey. In the years since the earthquake, the museum and the community had ample time to think about what they wanted from the de Young's next architect. With two successive buildings damaged by earthquakes, seismic safety was the overriding objective. Both the collections and educational programs were in need of more space, and better integration with the park was a widely held goal. Barnes was asked to put together a list of fifty architects to be sent a Request for Qualifications and Proposals that October. The competition was announced in the professional press. "The goal was geographical representation," said new de Young project director Deborah Frieden. "We wanted to have architects from Asia and Europe as well as the United States, and to include regional architects." Twenty-five from Barnes's list accepted the invitation and came to San Francisco in November for a tour of the site. Among these, a number were never seriously in the running, for reasons that were self-evident in the fall of 1998.[4]

The J. Paul Getty Museum had opened the previous December in Los Angeles, after fifteen years and at a cost of $1 billion. It is hard to overstate the degree of public fascination with this lavish undertaking and its architect, Richard Meier. The same year, Frank Gehry's Guggenheim Museum in Bilbao, Spain, had opened. The world had never seen anything like its exploding titanium-clad forms. Together, Meier's Getty and Gehry's Bilbao dominated the media, and were touted as the ultimate in what could be attempted in museum architecture. The de Young was being conceived in the shadow of these two tour-de-force museum buildings.

To have Richard Meier design the de Young was unthinkable. "We could not appear to have a little Getty," said Parker. Nor could Mario Botta be considered, since he had recently designed the city's other major art museum, the San Francisco Museum of Modern Art, in 1995. The Pei Cobb Freed firm had done the new San Francisco Main Public Library in 1996. Mexican architect Ricardo Legoretta had the commission for the Mexican Museum in San Francisco and had just completed the Tech Museum of Innovation in nearby San Jose. Billy Tsien's office in New York was thought not to be large enough to do the job. Among those who declined the museum's invitation were Frank Gehry and Steven Holl. From Italy, Renzo Piano pleaded an overload of work at that moment. From Japan, Arata Isozaki regretted that he could not attend the site visit. The short list of eight was made up of the Swiss team Herzog & de Meuron, Tadao Ando from Japan, Norman Foster from England, Ricardo Legoretta from Mexico, and the American offices of Cesar Pelli, Antoine Predock, Rafael Viñoly, and Pei Cobb Freed.

The museum accelerated the competition process, giving the firms six weeks to prepare for interviews in December. There were no formal site visits to the candidates' work: the thirteen-member selection committee would rely on interviews and slides submitted by the candidates.[5] Dean Harrison Fraker, the newly appointed head of the College of Environmental Design at the University of California at Berkeley, gave a lecture on the short-listed firms to prepare the committee for the interviews. Of those, five made it to the final round: Ando, Pelli, Predock, Viñoly, and Herzog & de Meuron.[6] Over the course of two rounds of voting by the committee, the field was narrowed to Ando, Predock, and Herzog & de Meuron. The committee had agreed that the decision must be unanimous. According to Wilsey: "I did not know who it would be until the third and final vote."

Tadao Ando had at that time built nothing in the United States, although his Modern Art Museum in Fort Worth and Pulitzer Foundation in St. Louis have since opened to critical praise. Revered among artists and in academia, Ando's museums in Kyoto and Osaka are international art shrines and were familiar to most of the committee members. Ando is admired for the simplicity and spiritual reverberations of his forms, as well as his philosophy that buildings should be interwoven with gardens and water. Given his focus on gardens, he was an attractive candidate to build in Golden Gate Park. There was also the appropriateness of his building next to the park's Japanese Tea Garden, which abuts the western edge of the new de Young museum.

Ando had a supporter in former *San Francisco Chronicle* owner Nan Tucker McEvoy, a principal donor to the de Young building campaign, who is an heir of the city's oldest media dynasty and the granddaughter of the museum's founder, Michael de Young. When Ando gave his presentation, according to Fraker, his natural reserve appeared to be a disadvantage. "He conveyed a powerful spiritual quality," Fraker said, but he was perceived as "too quiet for the political battles that lay ahead."[7] The committee had to consider how each design would be defended before a public body. Although such a defense was not required by law at that time, this did turn out to be the case when the Environmental Impact Report was challenged and its resolution put before the San Francisco Board of Supervisors. Ando's presentation showcased a waterfall in the museum's garden, and questions were raised about the energy costs of his water features and their impact on the constricted site.

Antoine Predock, a designer in the appealing maverick spirit of Wright and Gehry, had the advantage of being a Western regional architect who nevertheless is respected internationally. His substantial body of work, which includes important cultural institutions in Texas and the Southwest, is expressive and environmentally sensitive, and is perceived as Western in style without being kitsch. As such, Predock had a following in San Francisco and had long been considered a desirable candidate for an important building there. One of Stanford University's most admired buildings of the 1990s is a small addition he designed. On the committee, Predock had the support of real estate magnate Alfred Wilsey, whose wife was president of the board and sat on the selection committee. According to Fraker, Predock came across as confident in his presentation. "He stressed his ability to capture the poetic dimension of the institution, and give it regional expression."

Although Herzog & de Meuron were the youngest and least familiar to the committee, they had been enthusiastically recommended by the museum's architect Edward Larrabee Barnes, who knew their work from having served on the selection committee for the Museum of Modern Art in New York, for which they were among two runners-up to Yoshio Tanaguchi. In the interviews for the de Young commission, Herzog & de Meuron were the only architects who talked extensively about the museum's collections. According to Fraker, they did not propose a Disney-like thematic approach by the type of art, but promised to find a higher order of design that would express the collections. They also created the impression that whatever they came up with would be very well built, he said.

"They were perhaps even more reserved than Ando," Fraker said, "but they projected an intellectual intensity and curiosity. They were the young kids on the scene and they came across as caring tremendously about the museum. It was felt that they could deliver a synthesis of Ando and Predock: an exalted design that was also expressive of place. There were fears among the selection committee that their building would be too austere, too 'tough' for the public. But they overwhelmed the committee with their seriousness." According to Dede Wilsey, "I felt confident that if Pierre de Meuron ever had to go before the Board of Supervisors, he would be convincing."

HERZOG & DE MEURON

In 1999, Herzog & de Meuron were an adventurous choice for a city-owned museum in San Francisco. The museum was passing over the established generation represented by Tadao Ando and Renzo Piano in favor of architects still in their forties, known to the American public solely through the media. Herzog & de Meuron had succeeded brilliantly in the arena of paper architecture with their highly photogenic buildings and thought-provoking exhibitions. The writings and interviews of the firm spokesman, Jacques Herzog, had a wide audience of their own.[8] The firm's built work, however, consisted mainly of small projects in and around their home city of Basel, Switzerland. At least, that could have been the view from California. It would be another year before Herzog & de Meuron's adaptation of a London power station, the Tate Modern museum, gave them international visibility. It would be another two years before their recognition by the Pritzker Prize, and their selection for the expansion of the Walker Art Center in Minneapolis lay even further ahead. Moreover, Herzog & de Meuron lacked the sharply defined identity of the star architect. In the celebrity-oriented architecture culture of the 1990s, they were unusual in insisting on presenting themselves as a team—not just as a twosome, but later as a foursome with their younger partners Harry Gugger and Christine Binswanger.

Much that appeared promising about Herzog & de Meuron was attributed to their Swiss background. Although they made it a point to shrug off labels, including nationality, architecture critics were not hesitant to endow them with the virtues commonly ascribed to Swiss architecture in the 20th century: efficiency, concern for quality and correctness, and a sense of the suitable.[9] The latter can be seen in the strain of modesty that runs through Herzog & de Meuron's early work, relative to the 1980s tendencies toward the overscaled, the opulent, and the frivolously rhetorical.

Jacques Herzog and Pierre de Meuron were born in 1950 in Basel. A prosperous northern Swiss city bordering France and Germany, Basel has a tradition of fine craftsmanship dating from the Middle Ages. Europe's first public art collection was founded there in the sixteenth century, when the city was bequeathed the holdings of the

Tate Modern (2000), London

philosopher Erasmus. It is the home of the first museum of contemporary art, the Emmanuel Hoffman Foundation, established in 1933, and the world's leading fair for modern and contemporary art is held there each June. The city's deeply rooted culture of art patronage, collecting, and dealing has been invigorated in present times by the wealth of the pharmaceuticals industry. The headquarters and production plants of firms such as Novartis and Roche are fixtures of the city and its environs, and are nicknamed "the cathedrals" of Basel.

Herzog and de Meuron went to school in Basel and received their architecture degrees from the ETH, the Federal Institute of Technology in Zurich, in 1975. They often say that their work grows out of the student culture of the 1960s as it was transmitted to them by the architect and teacher Aldo Rossi, their professor at ETH. Rossi's insistence that the practice of architecture be defined anew, with its principles drawn solely from architecture itself, shaped the thinking of their European generation. This influence has been seen in the purity of intention with which Herzog & de Meuron approached their first buildings, disregarding symbolism, history, narrative, and theory to concentrate on the making of the object.[10]

Another formative experience was their youthful involvement with the art world. A famous story, so often told that it verges on a founders' myth, concerns the German artist Joseph Beuys. In 1977, Herzog and de Meuron had finished at the university but would not set up their architectural office for another year. The two traveled to Düsseldorf to visit their hero Beuys, and told him how they had designed costumes for a carnival club. The result was that Beuys provided costumes, including felt garments and copper instruments, for the carnival procession, which he himself joined. These artifacts were later exhibited at the Basel Kunstmuseum. Much has been written to associate Beuys's fabled work with felt, wood,

and copper with Herzog & de Meuron's intense interest in basic materials. Critics like to emphasize the architects' associations with artists, ranging from the studios they have designed for Remy Zaugg and the photographers Andreas Gursky and Thomas Ruff; to buildings incorporating curtains by Rosemarie Trockel and photographs by Ruff and Karl Blossfeldt; to an unbuilt scheme with Gerhard Richter, to name but a few.[11] From this roster of artists, however, one cannot deduce an alliance with any artistic movement or position, and those who try to do so are misguided. (Herzog & de Meuron have often been asked if they consider their own work to be art, which they deny, and what tendencies in art they wish to encourage.[12]) Rather, one should recognize that such artists are meaningful to the architects as individuals and colleagues, not collectively. Herzog & de Meuron reject classic hierarchies that place architecture at the top as "mother of the arts." They see architecture instead as part of society and its shared artistic enterprises, and assume that a painter or sculptor might make as valid a contribution to one of their buildings as a trained architect.

Herzog & de Meuron's early work does not fit within any of the architectural styles of its time, which is one of its virtues. Critics are fascinated by the way it accommodates conventionally defined opposites: minimalism and sensuousness, structure and cosmetics, rigor and playfulness, rationality and mystery. For an American client such as the de Young museum trustees, it was refreshing to work with architects who had launched their careers outside the debates that so preoccupied their generation in this country. Some of their peers have commented, with half-mocking envy, on the young Swiss architects' intellectual independence. In particular, it was noted, Herzog & de Meuron's freedom from "the Oedipus Complex" allowed them to borrow from the giants of modernism, such as Le Corbusier, Mies van der Rohe, and

Alvar Aalto, in certain projects, while elsewhere deviating from modernism in both letter and spirit. For example, Terence Riley has observed how Herzog & de Meuron's practice of combining clear, opaque, and translucent glazing, creating an atmosphere of mystery, defies the principles of transparency fundamental to Miesian modernism and flouts the master's dictum that glass must be either clear or opaque. What is enviable is that the architects are able to play out their debts to Le Corbusier and Mies, as well as to American minimalism, without this being a constraint on their other objectives.[13]

Herzog & de Meuron's work appeals powerfully to the eye and the emotions. As such, it seems to offer a way out of the sterility of minimalism and neo-modernist formalism, which was increasingly an advantage as the 1980s wore on. And while their work possesses reference and decoration, it did not share the limitations of postmodernist referentiality as practiced in the United States. The architects were at the opposite end of the ideological spectrum from postmodern historicism, with its quotations from past architecture. "Postmodernism was not on our agenda," Jacques Herzog has said.[14] This had a particular relevance for San Francisco, where a spate of downtown buildings in that vein had been erected, such as the new Main Library by Pei Cobb Freed and corporate work by Skidmore Owings & Merrill, Philip Johnson, and Robert A. M. Stern.

For the de Young, Herzog & de Meuron offered respectability on several fronts. They were revered in academia, where students studied their connections not only with Aldo Rossi, modernism, minimalism, and Swiss vernacular, but also with such subjects as Sigmund Freud, Andy Warhol, photography, and ethnography. They were a known quantity in the art world, having had exhibitions at the Centre Pompidou, the Museum of Modern Art in New York, and the Canadian Centre for Architecture. Yet

they had eluded art world labels, such as minimalist, high-tech, or light architecture, that might distance some elements of the San Francisco public. And if their lack of a signature style made it difficult to predict what a Herzog & de Meuron museum would look like, there was no question that it would be an antidote to an overkill of postmodern traditionalism in the city.

While the young Herzog & de Meuron were gaining a reputation as artist-architects, they were building with standard construction methods. In 1988, when schemes by Daniel Libeskind, Zaha Hadid, and Rem Koolhaas were presented in the Museum of Modern Art exhibition *Deconstructivist Architecture*, a commonly asked question was: "Can these designs be built? If so, at what cost?" This question haunted Libeskind's career for years. In the case of Koolhaas, it was being asked as late as 2004, when two commissions for major American museums, the Whitney Museum in New York and the Los Angeles County Museum of Art addition, fell through. But one never asked this question about Herzog & de Meuron. They were builders, products of Basel, with its cult of the well-made object. Later, as they were considered for projects in Asia, Britain, and the United States, their knowledge of both concrete and steel construction also gave them an advantage.

To the average observer, the hallmark of Herzog & de Meuron's buildings prior to the de Young was the sheer variety in their external appearance, the result of the architects' often-stated commitment to seeking new solutions. In speaking to clients, it is common for architects to utter the piety that every project is a fresh experiment. Herzog & de Meuron were remarkable in the degree to which they meant it. Projects are approached through what they call "investigations," which might involve research in outside fields such biology and geology. Remarkable, in turn, is the multiplicity of the representational tools with which they explore a project. These have ranged from sketches, folded paper, crude cardboard cutouts, rubber, wire mesh, metal, and polycarbonate figures, cheap paper models, and video stills to scaled, finished wooden models and elaborate full-scale maquettes, all made in their own workshop. Visitors to Herzog & de Meuron's Basel office pass through courtyards filled with these maquettes, ghostly garden sculpture evoking past buildings, such the rubble-filled wire cages for the Dominus Winery or the perforated copper panels for the de Young that serve as a gate.

By the mid 1990s, the Herzog & de Meuron firm was even more unusual in its relative independence from the computer, having remained immune to the seduction of morphing programs that swept through the profession in the 1990s. Computer programs are used to generate patterns for their decorated surfaces, such as the famous photo-printed polycarbonate panels at the Ricola Storage Facility in Mulhouse and the dimpled copper panels on the de Young, as well as to aid fabrication. But design is primarily done in what Pierre de Meuron calls "the old-fashioned way," with drawings and models. (Some of their

more recent projects use the computer in the design process, running parallel to other methods and techniques.)

The result, as one sees it in the buildings of Herzog & de Meuron's first fifteen years, is a parade of varied colors, patterns, materials, forms, and externally visible construction techniques. Often a question is being posed regarding issues of construction, the wit and profundity of which is evident chiefly to professionals. At their first house, the 1979 Blue House, an Yves Klein-inspired blue pigment vivifies the conventional stucco exterior. At the Stone House, local building stones are arranged within concrete frames, not to express structure but to create flat abstract patterns. At the Hebelstrasse Apartments in Basel, wood is used in the first of many layered facades in their work, in this case composed of a wall and attached balcony whose "cabinetlike" construction is subtly detailed, with slightly angled planes and twisting columns. A combination of clear, opaque, and translucent glass appears in the Goetz Gallery in Munich, where horizontal bands of glass and wood appear to reverse the classical order of weight, with the heavier timber panels suspended above the lighter glass portions, which seem to be pressed into the ground. The acrylic facade at the Ricola Storage Facility in Mulhouse is printed with a repeated image from a botanical photograph by Karl Blossfeldt. Bands of photographic images selected by Thomas Ruff are silkscreened on concrete, as well as glass, at the Eberswalde Library in Germany.

Among these works, the tour de force of beauty and ingenuity is the first SBB Signal Box in Basel, from 1994, housing computer switching systems for the Swiss railroad. Inspired by the Faraday Cage, the architects wrapped the apparently windowless building in strips of copper that twist subtly to allow light to pass through. The strips form a shimmering skin of shifting intensity, reflecting light

The copper gate, from mock-ups of the de Young facade panels, at the Herzog & de Meuron office, Basel

Top left: Stone House (1988), Tavole, Italy; top right: Blue House,
(1979), Oberwil, Switzerland; bottom: Apartment Building along
a Party Wall, Hebelstrasse (1987), Basel

Goetz Gallery (1991), Munich

Eberswalde Library (1999), Eberswalde, Germany

during the day and emitting light at night, when the Signal Box glows like a lantern. The American architect Philip Johnson made the trip to Basel in his nineties just to see the Signal Box. Another celebrated innovation is the gabion wall for the 1998 Dominus Winery in California's Napa Valley, where stones of differing sizes are held in place by wire containers, but arranged loosely enough that light shows through.

Through the 1990s, these facade systems became not only decorated, patterned, and colored, but layered, possessing depth and the capacity to alter light in the interior. Dappled light suffuses the inside of the Ricola Storage Facility building at Mulhouse and a latticework of light and shadow fills the interior of Dominus Winery. By 2003 a characteristically sensuous Herzog & de Meuron facade would turn the entire Laban Dance Centre near

DESIGNING THE NEW DE YOUNG

Above and opposite: Dominus Winery (1998), Yountville, California

Ricola-Europe Factory and Storage Building (1993), Mulhouse, France

London into an urban lantern. Both the building envelope and interior walls feature polycarbonate panels tinted blue, green, and violet, according to a method of coloration devised by the architects.

Among this profusion of materials, it is significant that Herzog & de Meuron do not observe conventional distinctions between the noble and the common. Nor, as Jacques Herzog points out, do their experiments with facade materials show a chronological progression, whether from commonplace materials to more inventive ones, or from organic to synthetic. "We do not move from more traditional materials in early projects to more modern materials in recent projects," he said, "as if to evolve toward better and better materials. The concept of each project and the quality of each project makes it contemporary or not, nothing else."[15]

By 1998 a sufficient number of themes had emerged within Herzog & de Meuron's output that the de Young building committee could imagine what their museum might look like. The powerful roofline with a cantilevered canopy is repeated at the Ricola facilities in Laufen and Mulhouse, the Pfaffenholz Sports Center outside Basel, and then at the new de Young. The strategy of slightly bending the facade appears at the early Plywood House, the Hebelstrasse Apartments, and the Ricola offices in Laufen. A horizontal glass volume, functioning as a lantern and source of indirect overhead light, is a feature of Tate Modern, the Goetz Gallery, and the Basel Railroad Engine Depot.

A constant in Herzog & de Meuron's work has been sensitivity to their buildings' settings. Their Basel work is commended for its harmony with the textures of their native city. In more recent years it has become apparent that wherever their work is, it fits beautifully. The Dominus Winery in Napa Valley and the Laban Dance Centre outside of London are striking for the way they enhance

The polycarbonate panels of the Ricola-Europe facade are silkscreened with a Karl Blossfeldt botanical photograph.

and poeticize their surroundings. Critics have refused to call Herzog & de Meuron contextualists—nor are they, in the literal sense. The setting is never the overriding determinant of their designs. Attention to context informs both details, however, such as the encouragement of local mosses on the concrete facade of the Ricola Storage Facility at Mulhouse, and grand strategies, such as the orientation of Tate Modern's top-floor public spaces toward the River Thames. Especially applicable to the de Young's situation

in Golden Gate Park is their use of orientation and apertures to define an open landscape as seen from inside the building, whether it is the semi-industrial margins of London from the Laban Dance Centre or the vineyard-covered hills of Napa Valley from Dominus Winery. A low-budget building from 2003, the Laban is remarkably ambitious in dealing with its setting, establishing grand axial vistas of the one landmark, a historic church, in this bleak neighborhood of council housing and industrial buildings.

But when the de Young was making its choice in 1998, critics were uncertain about the future direction of Herzog & de Meuron. Their architecture was still seen as one of surfaces. Their buildings were boxes, to the exteriors of which they applied enormous ingenuity and skill. From an American perspective, it is tempting to think of their work as a fulfillment of the "decorated shed" ideal promoted in 1974 by the Philadelphia polemicist and architect Robert Venturi. Venturi's own sheds, however, including warehouse retail outlets, were decorated with a very different type of imagery that was consciously imitative of Pop Art and drawn from advertising, movie stills, and sports scoreboards. This popular culture repertoire is employed by some of Herzog & de Meuron's peers, such as Koolhaas and his imitators. In using Karl Blossfeldt's 1928 botanical photograph or a 2001 Thomas Ruff photo collage to decorate the facades of their buildings, Herzog & de Meuron's aim is not communication with a mass audience, as Venturi and his followers professed in the 1970s and was inherent in their notion of the facade as billboard. Twenty-five years later, Herzog & de Meuron's figurative facades address a different audience, for whom the content of decoration may be arbitrary, and whose other concerns with the building's skin render the billboard analogy problematic.

Yet for Herzog & de Meuron in 1998, there remained the problem of the box, that is, how they might replace

Ricola Marketing Building (1998), Laufen, Switzerland. The textiles were designed in collaboration with Rosemarie Trockel and Adrian Schiess.

Laban Dance Centre (2002) was built on abandoned land along
Deptford Creekway, Lewisham (southeast London).

Railroad Engine Depot (1996), Basel

it in the next phase of their work, beginning with the de
Young commission. Their early reliance on the box had
been consistent with their roots in American minimalism,
for which the container is the basic structural unit. It was
unarguably appropriate for industrial buildings, among
them the Basel Railroad Engine Depot, the buildings
for Ricola, and Dominus Winery, which are, after all,
warehouses and production plants. Nevertheless, skeptics
wondered what Herzog & de Meuron's undeveloped
interiors boded for larger projects.[16] Tate Modern,
an adaptation of an existing structure carried out on
a stringent budget, did little to answer this question for
a client such as the de Young. Its dense London site was
a far cry from the blank slate of Golden Gate Park.[17] As to
the question of how these architects would approach
anything more complicated than a shed, let alone a well-
funded cultural building with a complex program, the jury
was still out when they were being considered for the San
Francisco museum. As we have learned since, the de Young
design coincided with new directions in Herzog & de
Meuron's work—seen also in the Ricola Headquarters, the
Prada store in Tokyo, and the project for Tenerife—toward
polygonal form and irregularly angled interiors, and an
ever more sophisticated handling of light and its effects.

What was encouraging about Herzog & de Meuron
in 1998, just before this turning point in their career,
was what can only be called their attitude, a combination
of seriousness, correctness, and confidence, fueled by an
appealing desire to please. What critics read as paradoxes
or tensions in their work, be they real or not, impressed the
critics because they gave them something to think about,
and often an occasion to change their minds. Herzog & de
Meuron's work had to overcome a cultural resistance to
admiring architecture that is unapologetically beautiful.
With its glowing light, subtle color, decoration, and
mystery, their work is an argument for pleasure in

Prada Shop and Offices (2003), Tokyo

Top: Sketch by Pierre de Meuron, 1999
Above: Nearing completion in April 2005

architecture. They are candid about their intentions on this score: "We want to make a sensual architecture," said Jacques Herzog, "an architecture that can't be experienced by the intellect alone."[18] If for nothing else, Herzog & de Meuron's work was exciting for revealing and questioning the architecture culture's prejudice against pleasure.

THE DESIGN AND BUILDING PROCESS

The de Young museum, as a new visitor to San Francisco's Golden Gate Park sees it from a distance, is a sleek horizontal building, indeterminate in color, set against a stand of tall trees. At one end, a tower rises from the slightly curving roof. At the other, a massive overhang juts out. But some who remember the old de Young Museum, which was torn down in 2002, may see something else again: a bold architectural statement. For more than one hundred years, a group of ornate Spanish Colonial and Egyptian Revival-style buildings stood on this spot. Their image lingers in the mind. The new de Young occupies a smaller footprint than the museum it replaced, but that does not soften its impact: It announces itself as an example of the new architecture, circa 2005.

As the museum was under construction in the winter of 2004, its architects looked back on an undertaking that had gone on for nearly six years, beginning even before they received the commission in January 1999. "The de Young was the largest project in our office for five years," Pierre de Meuron recalled. "This gave us so much time to experiment. It was a great luxury. So many of our recent ideas were developed in the years we had to work on the de Young."[19]

The years of experiment to which he refers were not devoted to basic concepts, however. These date from the very beginning. Between January and April 1999 all of the governing ideas for the museum were developed, following the architects' examination of the site the previous fall, when they received the brief of doubling the space of the

existing museum. "The initial concept still works," says Jacques Herzog, "because it was derived from the givens." And what were these givens? "The given was the park," he said. "Tradition and nature had to be foremost. The white box would not be the solution."

Everyone in the museum world knows what architects mean by the white box, often called the white cube.[20] It was the ubiquitous gallery type from the 1970s until the 1990s, when it began to give way to more expressive freeform galleries, Frank Gehry's Guggenheim Museum in Bilbao offering the ultimate example. But what could Herzog mean by the givens of nature? Obviously, there was a desire to take advantage of being in a park, instead of downtown, a location considered at one time. There were factors particular to the Northern California landscape: its topography, vegetation, weather, and light. More speculatively, the architects discerned a resonance between the natural world and the art to be housed, given the growing proportion of art from Africa, Oceania, and the Americas in the collections of the de Young museum. Commonly made of natural materials, many of these works were sacred objects in their cultures and were never intended to be displayed in formal indoor settings. As Jacques Herzog put it: "These objects belong to nature. We wanted to emphasize that."

The architects' first notion was to literally immerse the museum in nature by creating a set of pavilions surrounded by gardens. The architecture of each pavilion would express the regional origin of the art within. An earlier rendition of a garden pavilion, Herzog & de Meuron's 1992 Goetz Gallery, set amid birches and pines in a residential section of Munich, had produced one of their most admired buildings. But one must remember that this was 1999, barely a year after the much-heralded opening of the Getty Center in Los Angeles, where pavilions were used to break up the $1 billion construction project into comprehensible architectural units. Designing, as it were, in the shadow of Richard Meier's Getty, the pavilion model was not likely to be followed in San Francisco.

Vestiges of Herzog & de Meuron's pavilion scheme for the de Young exist in very early paper cutouts and models. "The pavilion idea just slipped away," said Herzog & de Meuron project architect Ascan Mergenthaler. "We worried about how we would represent these regional cultures without the risk of Disney-like architectural clichés. So we bracketed the pavilions under one roof. We came to prefer a prominent all-embracing roof, under which these cultures are symbolically united, rather than emphasizing separateness." The practical drawbacks to pavilions were considerable, including the logistics of multiple entrances and the difficulty of base-isolating separate buildings, the preferred engineering procedure for ensuring seismic stability. The site is narrow, bounded by the Music Concourse, John F. Kennedy Drive, and the Japanese Tea Garden. Cost and the restricted site favored a rectangular structure on a reduced footprint of the old museum. A two-story building was dictated by height limitations in the park and the desire for overhead daylight in certain galleries. The resulting bulk would have to be diminished by various architectural strategies, as we shall see.

Distinguishing features of the de Young as it stands today—including the strong roofline, the cantilever, the tower, the central court, and the two-story form—were all on the agenda at the first design meeting in Basel. As part of the concept plan, they were presented to the museum's Board of Trustees in June 1999. The tower and courtyard were proposed, in part, in the hope of reminding people of the old de Young, whose tower, Hearst Court, and entry court were among its most familiar and beloved features. "We wanted to give their tower and courtyard back to the people of San Francisco," said Jacques Herzog. "The cantilever had to be there to balance the tower, and both work to elongate the box." Indeed, the rationale for posing the vertical line of the tower against the strong horizontals of roof and cantilever is apparent in Pierre de Meuron's sketches from those very early meetings. His 1999 sketch showing the roof, tower, and cantilever is a convincing composition and remains a useful tool for admiring the finished building.

Meanwhile, in 1999, key players had been added to the team. The landscape architect Walter Hood, a specialist in public parks and community design from nearby Oakland, would work on the open courtyards that became a central feature of the museum interior, as well as the sculpture garden and exterior landscape design. Herzog & de Meuron had helped choose the San Francisco firm of Fong & Chan Architects as the local architects to manage cost and functional aspects of the design, including code specifications. Theirs was a crucial role in the age of global architectural practice. The Swiss architects had at that time only one experience of building in the United States, the Dominus Winery, a small private project. Now their design ideas would have to be made buildable in San Francisco, with the specific challenge of construction in a seismic zone, where the previous museum had fallen victim to earthquake damage.

In April 1999, Pierre de Meuron traveled to San Francisco to present the architects' preliminary concepts before an audience of 200 trustees, staff, and community leaders in the museum auditorium. Using maps of the park and the city, he described their goal of relating the new de Young to the immediate context of Golden Gate Park, to the larger context of the skyline and street grid, and to regional landmarks such as the towers of the Golden Gate Bridge. He assured the audience that the new building would retain its formal role as one of two museums flanking the classical Music Concourse, with its terraces

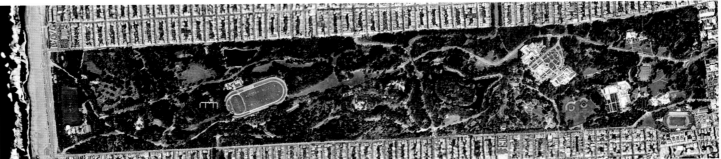

San Francisco: the Golden Gate Bridge at top, the Pacific Ocean at
left, and Golden Gate Park at center left (top photo) and in detail
(below)

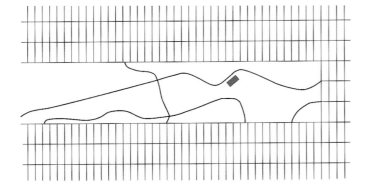

and rows of trees on an axis with the historic Spreckels Temple of Music. De Meuron gestured with two hands to demonstrate how the new museum would be more fully integrated with the park, showing how they would interlock like "fingers." By the time de Meuron returned to San Francisco the following June to present the conceptual plan, the building's "fingers" had taken the form of three horizontal bands, separated at the ends by triangular openings representing the incursion of the park. The pavilions, as can be seen from the progression of paper cutouts, had been consolidated into the three bands, and the gardens had been internalized as long, narrow landscaped courtyards that ran in between them.

Ascan Mergenthaler describes how the Basel design team produced this tripartite plan, working in one dimension with paper cutouts and drawings. They were guided by a document they had prepared analyzing the collection by number, type, scale, and significance of the objects to be housed. "First we established a band of program, then a band of park, then a band of program, of park, and of program. Then we began assigning the galleries, public spaces, support spaces, and so on, to the program bands. As we went on, we developed a conceit of switches and contact points to indicate where the program bands intersect. A crucial decision was establishing the

central distribution point, where visitors would cross from all of the levels and wings of the building." The breakthrough at this stage was finding that point at top of the main staircase. At that moment, Wilsey Court, which had been entertained conceptually as a means for evoking the demolished Hearst Court, found its function as the switch point on the main floor.

The three-band scheme that de Meuron showed in the public meetings was a synthesis of such working tools. As such, it was never intended, of course, to convey the style or materials of the building that would replace the old Spanish Colonial Revival de Young, with its familiar beige stucco and red tile. But the scheme did impart crucial information that should have gone a long way to reassure traditionalists in the audience. The museum would still be symmetrically aligned with the classical Music Concourse. It would still balance the California Academy of Sciences building directly across the way. Although at 293,000 square feet it would have twice the floor area of the old museum, providing the desired increase in galleries and education facilities, its footprint was 20 percent smaller, which augured well for its impact on the park. Daylight and park views, conspicuously lacking in the old museum, would now be provided. And if any in the audience had counted on hearing more about what the building would look like, they did not speak up. Those who did speak were impressed by the sincerity that de Meuron projected, and

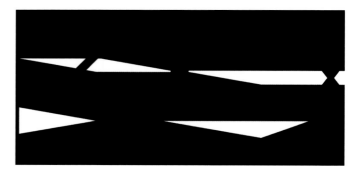

The de Young's position in the park, at an angle to the street grid

The "three-band" design as a logo

by the Swiss firm's efforts to familiarize themselves with San Francisco and the region.

A bold abstraction of the three bands was proposed as the logo for the fundraising campaign then getting underway, but rejected as too difficult to read as a building. Yet what single image could effectively represent the building to the public at this early stage? It was a vexing question. When more recognizably architectural sketches, depicting the tower and facade, were released to the press in June 1999, the unintended consequences were unfortunate. As they were reproduced in the *San Francisco Chronicle* and in *Architecture* magazine, for example, the renderings showed the building's exterior walls as a shadowy gray.[21] It was not explained that this color was merely a placeholder for a palette of materials that had barely been discussed. A spate of cartoons, columns, and letters to the editors lambasted the new de Young for its cold, glass-and-steel corporate architecture.[22] The new de Young was compared to a shopping mall and an aircraft carrier, analogies that stuck. This premature critique was to haunt the development of the design for the next three years.

The following August and September, Pierre de Meuron returned to San Francisco to present the conceptual plan to more than 500 citizens at two public workshops. The museum had held public meetings on rebuilding over the previous two years. Now that they had Herzog & de Meuron on board, they were giving the community an opportunity to hear directly from the architects. Standing alongside Fine Arts Museums director Harry Parker before the crowd in the Hearst Court, de Meuron once again outlined the architects' contextual rationale, emphasizing the themes of nature and openness to the park. In the question period, most comments were encouraging. Speakers from the university and architecture communities commended the boldness, internationalism, and cultural neutrality they saw in the Herzog & de Meuron plan. But they were drowned out by hostile voices. Looking perplexed, the architect faced speakers who were impatient with the discussion of urban planning issues, who had come ready to debate design. Some challenged the idea of a tower; others questioned the interior courtyards and windows on the park; others deplored the loss of the Hearst Court. Incited by the rumors of an all-glass exterior, some demanded to know then what the facade material would be.

Curiosity about the facade was to be expected. Herzog & de Meuron had earned their reputation with buildings with beautiful surfaces, often radically innovative in their materials and construction. What could be more unusual than the rock-filled wire cages that formed the skin of Dominus Winery? This was the example of Herzog & de Meuron's work nearest at hand, and was familiar to many in the audience. Of course they would wonder what the skin of the de Young might be. Hard put to comment, de Meuron said they wanted to use natural materials and were even considering wood. Pressed as to the type of wood, he mentioned redwood. This answer unleashed further objections: that redwood was not sufficiently sturdy or permanent, not formal enough for a civic building, and too tedious as the covering for a building of such immensity. These were the same questions about redwood that would be brought up in the architects' discussions with the building committee.

For Herzog & de Meuron, the idea of redwood was a logical response to Bay Area tradition. The architects were conversant with the first Bay Region Style, dating from the 1890s, and revered its great works in redwood, such as Bernard Maybeck's Christian Science Church in Berkeley. They had visited contemporary redwood houses in Marin County when they first came to Northern California in 1994 to work on the Dominus and the Kramlich Residence

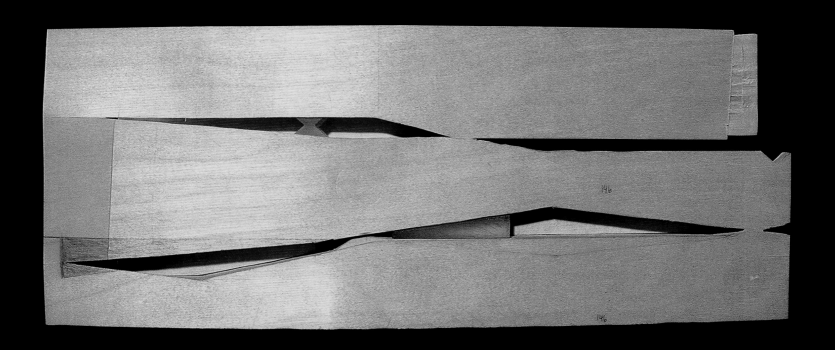

From pavilions to a single building: early models (top, left to right)
show interlocking pavilions coalescing into three horizontal bands
divided by narrow courtyards (bottom left); arrows in the model
(bottom right) indicate "switch points" where circulation paths meet.

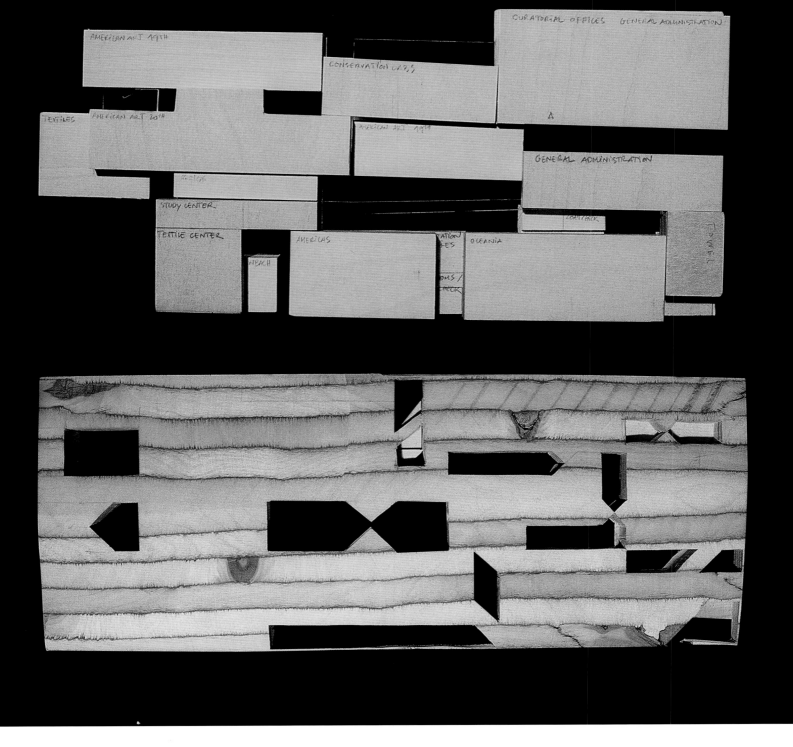

projects in Napa, and were aware of the availability and longevity of recycled old redwood. In 1999 Parker took de Meuron to see the little-known redwood masterpieces on the Russian River at the Bohemian Grove, including the unusual Maybeck Chalet and Mullgardt Art Gallery. More to the point, they had taken cues directly from redwood structures in Golden Gate Park. The architects often stayed at a museum trustee's house at Ocean Beach, where their morning run would take them by the Windmill at the western border of the park, facing the Pacific. They cite the Windmill's use of copper and redwood as an example of

how they wished to play out a larger definition of the natural that involved not only materials but processes.

"We were looking for a material that ages," Jacques Herzog would recount later, "and one we could allow to age naturally. The Windmill's wood and copper, as they weather, come closer together in color." The architects had initially talked about the facade as a patchwork of materials, which might include wood, glass, and possibly metal. An abiding issue was the bulk of the museum building, which could be de-emphasized through various strategies: by curving the roof, bending the facade, or

Large model showing second-floor galleries, conservation labs, and interior courtyards

cladding the building in contrasting materials. One could use materials that would blend into the setting: a stand of tall trees behind and to the east, and the foliage and wooden structures of the Japanese Tea Garden to the west. The proposed wood and copper were materials that would soften in color over time, creating a mottled rather than uniform surface, and increasingly approximate the greenish-brown palette of the surroundings.

Herzog & de Meuron's most forcefully stated rationale for the facade, however, was that the identities of the different collections should be expressed on the exterior of the building. As an institution, the de Young had been from its inception an eclectic museum, with wide-ranging holdings including textiles, graphic arts, decorative arts, and American art from the seventeenth to the nineteenth century. Beginning in the 1980s, there was an emphasis on acquiring twentieth-century and contemporary art as well as the art of Africa, Oceania, and the Americas, referred to within the museum by the name of the curatorial department, AOA. By 2005, the AOA material would comprise a quarter of the de Young's collection and occupy more than one-third of the permanent gallery space in the new building. The architects themselves had a longstanding interest in ethnography and the art of indigenous cultures. They professed a particular affinity for the de Young's growing AOA collections. "We wanted these galleries to be expressed as a special space on the facade," said Mergenthaler. In early elevations, the presence of the AOA collections on the south side of the building facing the park is indicated by redwood siding and large windows, implying the ties with nature that concerned the architects.

Even though the architects had intended to use recycled old redwood, rather than newly cut trees, they rejected redwood as a material once the economics were apparent. "There were concerns about how to maintain it, how to reseal it, about supply," said Mergenthaler. Wood was but

Top right: Golden Gate Park's Dutch Windmill, which has redwood shingles and copper fittings, appealed to the architects for its use of materials that age naturally.

Above: The Japanese Tea Garden (1894) borders the de Young's Barbro Osher Sculpture Garden.

one of the materials considered in a series of experiments with cladding that continued for three years, moving from glass, copper, and redwood siding, to open copper wire mesh, to embossed copper panels, to perforated copper panels, and, finally, to copper panels that are both dimpled and perforated. The saga of the facade progressed from the workshops and courtyards of Herzog & de Meuron in Basel to the laboratories and factories of A. Zahner Company, in Kansas City, where the copper sheets were eventually made. The facade represents the longest and most visible instance of how the design for the de Young developed over time. It also best illustrates how Herzog & de Meuron work. They are tireless in the exploration of their options, fabricating samples and building one-to-one mock-ups of details, drawing from a wide range of materials: natural and synthetic, luxurious and commonplace, and including readymade parts.

The museum interior was discussed in preparation for the presentation of the schematic design to the de Young trustees in June 2000. Its design involved the large models for which Herzog & de Meuron's workshop is also known. The disposition of public spaces and circulation was informed by the philosophical goal of linking the outdoors and indoors, and the inherent challenge of admitting light into a building of this size. Major corridors were run alongside the glass walls of interior courtyards, allowing for the play with light and reflection that is the architects' forte. Much critical commentary is devoted to the effects Herzog & de Meuron achieve by layering glass and polycarbonate and joining windows and walls at acute and obtuse angles.[23] The result can be multiple reflections, the blurring or accentuating of sight lines, or the confusing of distinctions between windows and walls, and between what lies ahead and what behind. This is how Mergenthaler describes the experience of entering the museum: "Visitors will walk from the entry court alongside the glass wall of the interior courtyard. The glass is set at an angle. So they see reflections of the spaces they have just left, at the same time they have the actual views ahead toward the galleries and sculpture garden."

From the beginning, there was a determination on the part of the architects to be innovative with some of the galleries. In many museums known for their imaginative architecture, the galleries remain formulaic. One sees the hand of the architect everywhere but in the galleries. "Everyone is so tired of these dreary museum interiors," said Jacques Herzog. In 1999 and 2000, Parker led discussions between the architects and the museum's curators on the scale, shape, lighting, and symbolism of individual galleries. At design meetings, there was a color chart showing hundreds of the de Young's objects at scale, from the smallest—a single spoon in the collection of American silver—to the largest, a Maya stela and a seventy-five-foot totem pole. It was decided that conventional rectangular spaces would be used only for the art of Western derivation, such as the twentieth-century and contemporary galleries, which would be classically shaped, with high ceilings. Galleries for American art of the seventeenth century to the nineteenth century would have lower ceilings, the extra space allowing for skylights. A range of historical skylighting conventions, including the cupola, were explored, leading to the choice of the extruded lantern, or lightbox.

In keeping with the architects' view of the African and Oceanic collections as "belonging to nature," the galleries housing them would be freer in form. "We wanted to be inventive," said Mergenthaler, "to go beyond what the de Young had before." Instead of white boxes, those galleries would be more like sweeping passageways, with lofty ceilings and walls set at angles, and with generous windows giving onto courtyards and the park. "Since the windows in these galleries were so important," he said, "we mimicked

Herzog & de Meuron's San Francisco office, 2003. Around the model, left to right: architects Mark Loughnan and Ascan Mergenthaler, museum director Harry S. Parker III, and project director Deborah Frieden. At the back: Diana Ketcham and architect Jayne Barlow

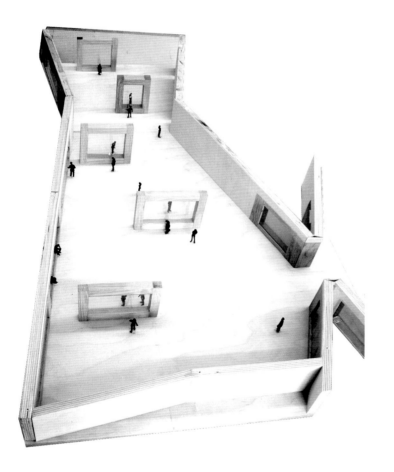

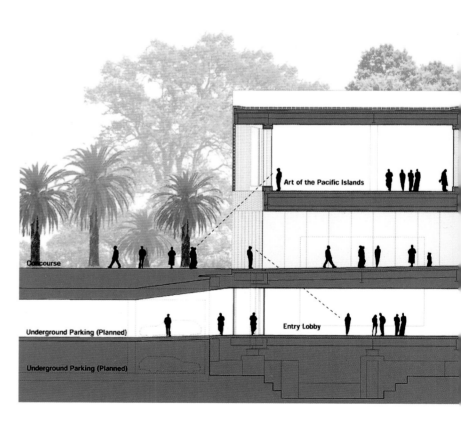

Top and above left: Models of the art of Oceania wing. In the built museum, the large windows (shown at right in the top illustration) are covered by a copper screen.

Above: A section from east to west showing the Art of the Pacific Islands (art of Oceania wing) on the second level

the shape of these windows in the display cases. When you look into the cases, are you looking inward or outward to the park? We wanted to encourage this type of confusion in the mind of the viewer. Are you looking at the object, or is the object looking at you?"

The position of the tall, freeform galleries informed the roofline. Observing the models, one grasps the meaning of the architects' contention that in their recent designs, as Jacques Herzog stated, "program and volume are one." Or, in common parlance, the overall form of the building is driven by the spaces within, rather than the reverse. The most common criticism of Herzog & de Meuron's very

early work was that they began with a box, then divided it up. With the de Young, they were demonstrating their ability to shape interior space.

The architects stress the importance of the roof at the de Young, calling it "the fifth facade." The roof is what one sees from the tower, as well as the compositional gesture that unifies the building as seen from everywhere else. The architects briefly considered a "green" roof, according to Mergenthaler. "It was something we would have explored for a building other than a museum, but we did not like the idea of earth and water above rooms containing art. It was not just the stories of famous leaking planted roofs. It felt

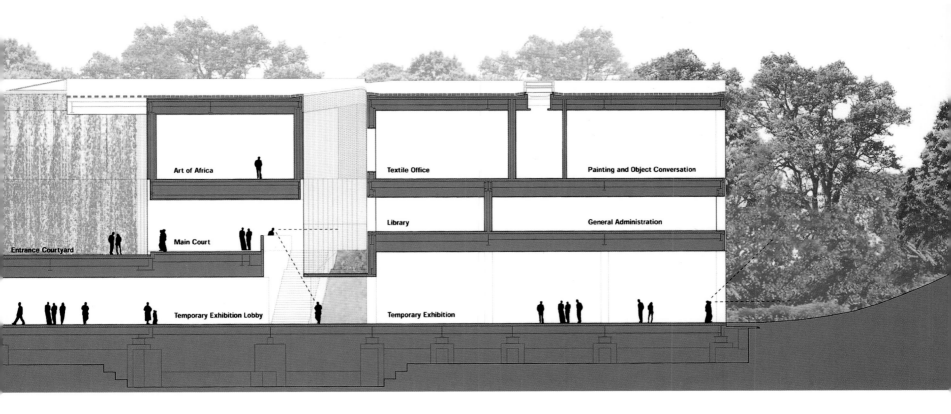

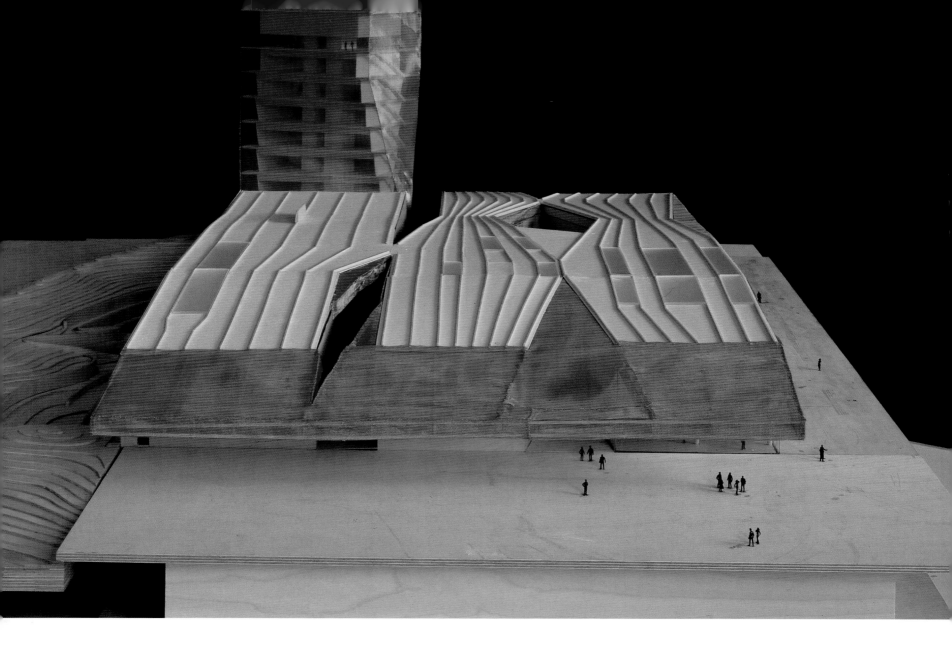

DESIGNING THE NEW DE YOUNG

Above and opposite: Models showing the copper roof, conceived as
the building's "fifth facade"

wrong in a visceral sense." (Kevin Roche's much admired 1969 Oakland Museum has been bedeviled by leaks from its roof gardens.) In years to come, this choice may loom as a significant one. The de Young will inevitably be compared to the other new museum in Golden Gate Park, architect Renzo Piano's addition to the California Academy of Sciences, which will have a green roof when it opens in 2008. The roof of the de Young was first conceived in wood, but the building committee favored copper over wood for its superiority in protecting the galleries underneath, as well as in maintenance and longevity.

A comparison of early models of the roof indicates how the banding emblem was carried through in the design process. One model shows the roof scored by thin slices, representing the openings over the interior courtyards, which divide the building into the three bands of program. In another model, this tripartite division is further articulated, with three roof bands undulating independently. In the last, the bands of the roof have coalesced into a single sloping roof, but the open areas above the courtyards have grown larger and more distinct in shape, including a great slice out of the canopy that extends over the western terrace.

In the completed museum, these openings, originally little more than two-dimensional markings on the surface of the roof, bring light deep into the building, with minimal exposure to the art. They also play a role in the high drama of light, shadow, and skyward views that informs the visitor's experience, especially from under the canopy. Triangular in shape, the canopy opening repeats the triangles of the interior courtyards. In the completed building, it throws a bold pattern of light across the western terrace, which, with its cafe tables overlooking the sculpture garden, is a major gathering place for visitors to the museum.

The tower is the other feature that underwent a marked design evolution, going through three main iterations

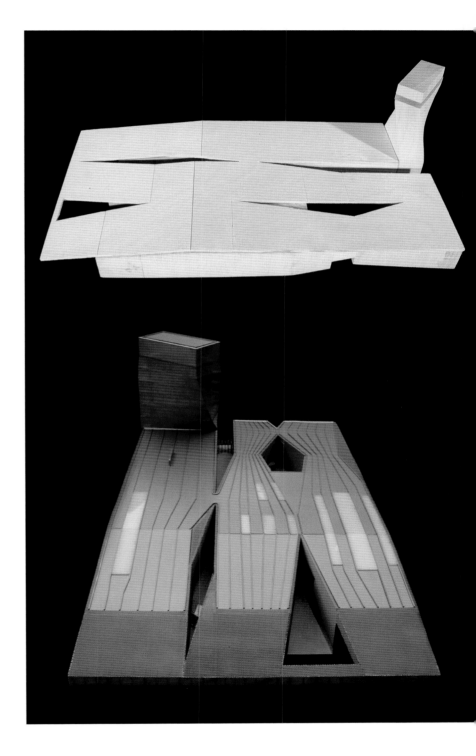

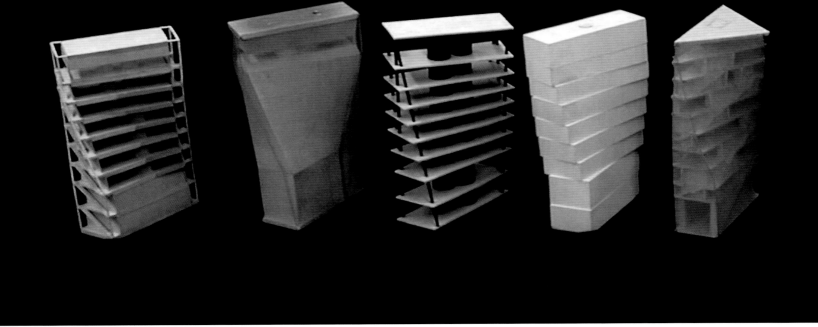

between 1998 and 2002. Among the most arresting and beautiful artifacts of the de Young's design process are the tower models in wire, foil, acrylic, paper, and metal, as well as computer-generated drawings and representations. The most artistic of these may be the tower modeled from mesh pantyhose. An asymmetrical tower appeared in the architects' entry as finalists for the New York MoMA competition in 1997, but the de Young tower had its own rationale. In concept, it was necessary to announce the presence of the museum, otherwise hidden in the park, on the San Francisco skyline and to make it a landmark on a par with the towers of the Golden Gate Bridge, the downtown skyscrapers, Coit Tower, and the Ferry Building.

Herzog & de Meuron's conceptual design specified that the top of the rectangular tower would twist away from the rectangular outlines of the building, aligning itself instead with the city grid. This ingenious and sophisticated contextual argument for a tower did not, however, say

where the tower would stand. "It could have been next to the tallest tree, or over the entrance, like the old tower," said Mergenthaler. Recognizing the dominance of the roof, the fifth facade, an early model has the tower as an extension of one corner of the roof, peeling up from the northeast edge of the building. Another issue, of course, was the engineering required for the twisted tower, which would stand in an earthquake zone.

A breakthrough in thinking about the tower was the decision to use its interior spaces for free educational activities, rather than staff offices. Parker wanted the tower to symbolize the museum's commitment to education. "Most museums hide their children's programs in the basement," said Parker, who insisted from the beginning that education have a prominent place in the new de Young, physically and symbolically. Hence the Education Tower. In keeping with the ideal of mingling the park and the museum, the design allows the public to walk through

The design of the tower evolved over a four-year period, from 1998 to 2002.

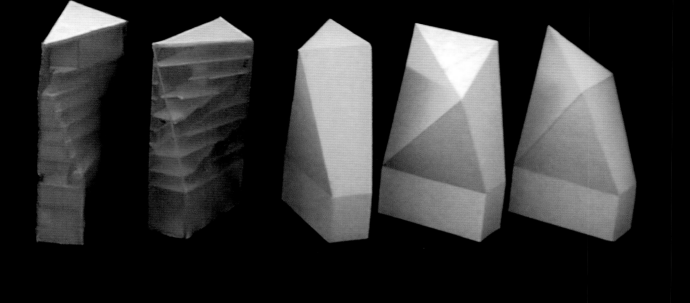

the ground floor to the tower and enjoy some services for free. This was intended to enhance the museum's efforts to attract new visitors and build its audience. "People can explore the museum a bit at a time," said Wilsey. "They might walk in from the park to use the shop or cafe, then come back to visit an exhibition that caught their eye."

The design of the de Young continued to evolve over several years. Some modifications were inherent to the undertaking, such as changes to untested cladding materials once they were studied. Others were inspired by responses to Herzog & de Meuron's ideas by museum staff, citizens' groups, and government agencies. When the initial design came in 20 percent over budget, as well as over program, the scale was reduced in the subsequent schematic design. There was ongoing give-and-take between value engineering studies and rising costs, with the construction budget eventually growing to $135 million. Scaling back meant that the footprint of 125,000

square feet was shrunk to 91,000, with the length of the building reduced from 520 feet to 420 feet. The tower was shortened from 160 feet to 144. (As a point of comparison, the old building's tower was slightly lower, at 125 feet, and its length greater, at 504 feet.) The striking cantilevered canopy at the western end of the building was shortened by one bay. "We had wanted it to extend out as far possible," said Mergenthaler, "to push it to the absolute limit of what the engineering allowed. So this was a compromise." An instructive convergence between the objectives of the designers, public opinion, and government procedures took place at the end of 2001, when it was discovered that the tower height was erroneously analyzed in the EIR calculations at 144 feet instead of the planned 160 feet. "We were aware of objections to the height and the architects were already working on changes to the tower," said project director Frieden. "They took the opportunity to proceed with these changes while bringing the height

down to 144 feet." With the revised tower height, the EIR
was approved by the San Francisco Board of Supervisors
in January 2002, the culmination of more than 200
meetings with city officials. Referring to the crucial role
of city politics over the many years Pierre de Meuron
worked on the de Young, the architect singled out the
approval as "the turning point in the design process."

Risk was inherent in the architects' determination to
experiment with materials for the skin. Not the least was
the risk of adverse criticism, as one idea after another
was revealed to the public. As an alternative to the initial
consideration of wood siding and glass, the architects
proposed a more unusual surface, copper mesh. The mesh
scheme triggered interest in the design community, where
many admired Dominus Winery's facade of wire mesh
and rock, and the filigree of light and shadow it produced
in the interior. "The mesh would have given depth and
movement to the building surfaces," said Harrison Fraker.
As the architects pursued this novel scheme, they had the
support of Parker, Wilsey, and the trustees on the building
committee. "It was very challenging for the client, but they
were with us," said Jacques Herzog. "We liked the softness
of mesh facing the park, and a facade that would move.
Then we realized that it was too risky. There was the public
reaction, that this resembled a chain-link fence. If this was
the connotation and the public didn't want it, we didn't
want it either." In February 2001, the architects surprised
building committee members who had gathered in Basel
with the news that the mesh solution had been abandoned.
As Mergenthaler describes their decision: "Then we
thought that the facade didn't have to be soft. It could
be more protective. So we thought of
shingles, which are applied to protect,
like the shingles at the Windmill.
In thinking of copper shingles,
we got to the copper panels."

The twisted tower rises 144 feet, nineteen feet higher than the tower
of the previous building. The top of the tower is oriented to align with
the street grid outside the park.

In early experiments with the skin, the transparency of the mesh concept was translated as a copper sheet with holes punched in it. In some versions, the copper panel was embossed with a pattern of circles that were not perforated. In their Basel workshop, the architects were already using a cheap metal panel with a dimpled surface for model building. "We enjoy finding a readymade material that can give rise to a sophisticated treatment," said Mergenthaler. "On these little panels, what we liked was the three dimensional effect of the dimples going in and out. It was an interesting texture. So we started embossing anything we could get our hands on. We had wooden tools for embossing made in our workshop and used them on a variety of materials."

Since they were considering copper, the architects had plastic panels made to scale, then painted them metallic copper. Future historians will note with amazement that the architects conceived the copper-panel solution without the assurance of being able to rely on computer production technologies. It is a testament to Herzog & de Meuron's confidence and habit of hands-on design that they began their research for the facade panels in their own workshop, without computers, before they knew how the panels would be mass-produced. Nor was it known how the facade would be assembled. Deborah Frieden became responsible for ensuring the constructability of the copper facade and that the custom assembly could be warranted. In 2001, an international search led her to A. Zahner Company in Kansas City. A family firm specializing in architectural metals, Zahner has worked with architects and artists such as Frank Gehry and sculptor Martin Puryear, and is known for high-profile metal-clad buildings such as Gehry's Frederick R. Weisman Art Museum at the University of Minnesota in Minneapolis. Working with project architects Fong & Chan and the contractors, Zahner developed the facade. They devised the structural system for attaching,

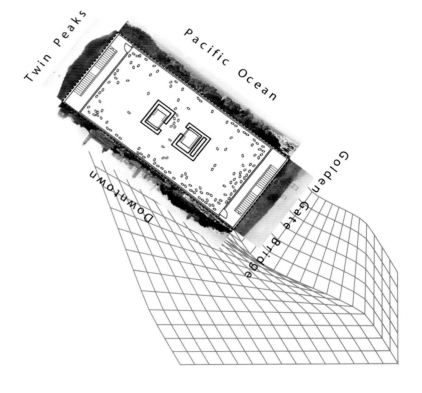

The public observation floor at the top of the tower provides panoramic views of the city.

1067867166

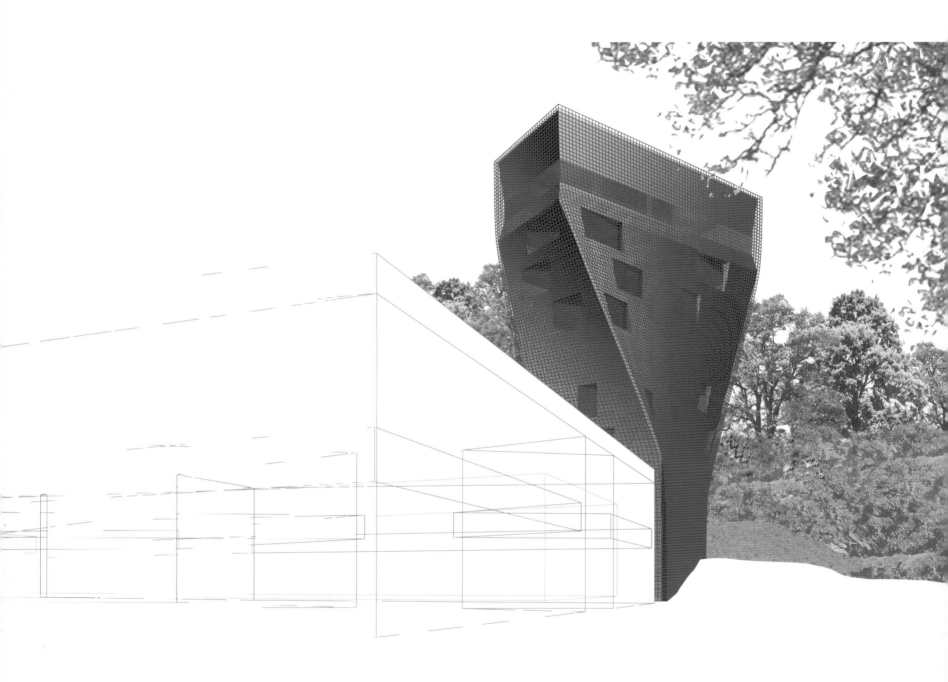

Above and opposite: Computer renderings show the twisting form
of the 144-foot tower from multiple angles.

architects' design. A computerized engineering system enabled the 7,200 panels to be individually cut, punched, and embossed according to the architects' directions. The pattern was derived from pixilated photographs Herzog & de Meuron had taken of trees and bushes in Golden Gate Park.

Herzog & de Meuron like to point out that they were attracted to dimpled copper by its essential properties, having to do with aesthetics and longevity, rather than by what they were then hearing about the new possibilities in metal fabrication technology. The de Young was designed at a time, the late 1990s, when the fashion for metals was on the rise. Metal skins became identified with the most daring, expressive, and technically advanced new architecture, a result of the sensation caused by the opening of the 1993 Weisman Art Museum, with its faceted stainless-steel facade, the titanium-clad 1997 Guggenheim Bilbao, and the 2004 Disney Concert Hall in Los Angeles, which uses steel. Titanium is also associated with the risk of unexpected maintenance problems, which arose at Bilbao.

 Copper, by contrast, is an age-old building material with established properties. Prized for its beauty and durability, copper has been used to cover large roofs since the Renaissance and had re-emerged in Europe in the 1990s to clad entire structures. Herzog & de Meuron had used copper successfully on their most critically admired early building, the 1994 Signal Box in Basel, with its skin of twisting copper strips. Still, they had never used copper on a building of the size and bulk of the 293,000-square-foot de Young, where each of the 7,200 copper panels is individually patterned and shaped. A total of 950,000 pounds of copper was used, making it the largest copper-clad building in the world. The architects knew how copper

in the atmosphere. Fears that the copper skin would remain unpleasantly shiny were unfounded. The skin had weathered to a subdued brownish shade by the spring of 2005, six months before the opening.

The architects have continued to work with metal panels. At the 2003 Schaulager art storage building in Basel, a simple scheme of identical panels is used on the interior of the theater. At the 2005 expansion of the Walker Art Center in Minneapolis, the tower's aluminum facade is made up of uniformly textured panels, unlike the de Young's, all of which are different.

The story of what was termed the New Museum at the turn of the twenty-first century is marked by tensions between ambitious architecture and other institutional objectives, including the demands of the art. The architecturally adventurous new de Young will contribute its own chapter to that story. For example, after proposing a huge bank of windows for the second-floor wing of Oceanic art, which would overlook the park and give articulation to the entrance facade, the architects had to negotiate with museum curators and conservators worried about light damage to sensitive art works. "The result was to keep the windows," Ascan Mergenthaler said, "but for us to design a louvered copper screen that would extend in front of them, protecting the art." With the proposal of an overall copper skin for the building, the architects challenged the museum trustees to be adventurous. "It was the biggest risk for the museum," he said, "but we were able to win their support. We came to agree that copper was the best solution for a unique building in this fantastic park."

The architects experimented with several variations of textured,
punched, and dimpled metal panels, embossing them with tools
made in their own studio.

DESIGNING THE NEW DE YOUNG

Pixilated photographs of the tree canopy in the park were used
as a point of departure for the design of the museum's copper skin.
A computer program transformed the images into an abstract
pattern of dimples, bumps, and perforations.

The 7,200 copper panels for the facade were fabricated at A. Zahner
Company in Kansas City, Missouri.

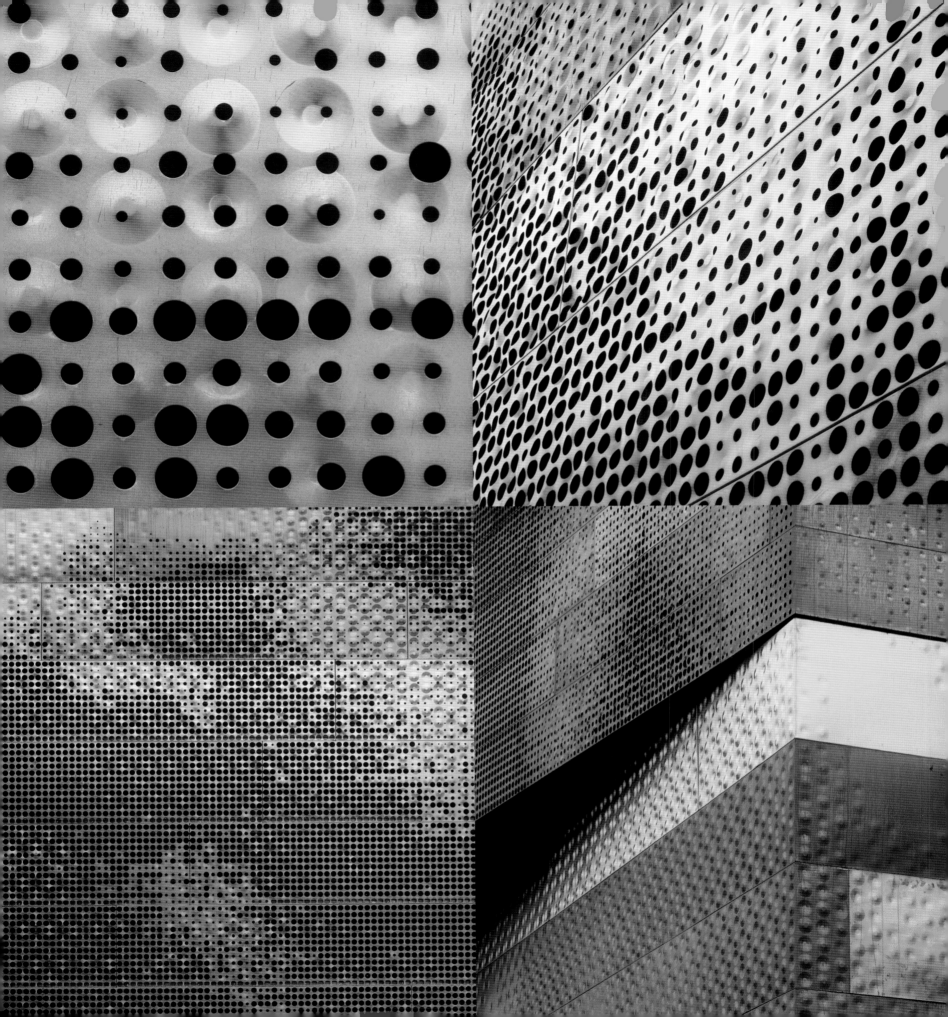

04

In 1999, Fong & Chan Architects, a San Francisco-based office led by partners Chiu Lin Tse-Chan and David Fong, was brought on board for the crucial role of principal architects, responsible for executing Herzog & de Meuron's design for the new de Young Museum. Known for combining design excellence with high-quality construction drawings, the firm oversaw engineering and constructability issues, code compliance, and material and product specification.

Some of the challenges facing Fong & Chan Architects were inherent in the design. "Herzog & de Meuron's free-flowing cultural pavilions connected by linked stairs and hallways make for exciting dynamic spaces," said Chiu Lin Tse-Chan. "At the same time, they create particularly complex geometries. One of our greatest challenges was to translate these geometries into two-dimensional drawings that could be readily understood and built." Equally difficult was conforming the design to American building codes, which differ greatly from those in Europe. A further, overriding challenge was building on sandy soil in a seismically active zone. These realities influenced the design and construction of the de Young in ways not readily apparent to museum visitors.

BASE ISOLATION

A method of designing structures to better withstand earthquake vibrations, base isolation is the preferred foundation system for achieving seismic safety in San Francisco's large public buildings. It was essential that the new de Young's structure provide a superior level of protection. Fong & Chan oversaw the design of the base isolation system developed by Rutherford & Chekene, structural engineers.

The foundation is separated from the building above it by devices that allow the base to move independently and absorb vibrations so they are not transmitted to the structure. The entire steel frame of the museum rests on seventy-six elastomeric bearings and seventy-six slider bearings, allowing a total horizontal movement of up to three feet in any direction.

The building is surrounded by a moat, three and one-half feet wide at its minimum, that will accommodate the displacement during an earthquake. The moat also separates the three-story main building from its nine-story tower and adjacent underground parking garage, which are conventional fixed-base buildings.

"Honoring the design intent while developing sound solutions for earthquake safety was a huge technical challenge," said David Fong. His firm's job was to integrate, then conceal, these seismic safety features. Fong & Chan project manager Nuno Lopes likes to point out that visitors coming into the museum will unknowingly walk across the moat, concealed by stone pavers or other landscaping materials. "The building is like a jigsaw puzzle," Lopes said. "The interlocking parts can be displaced and disconnected during a seismic event, but eventually all the parts come back together in their original static state."

The design concept called for the park to come right up

View from the north of the cantilever and the nearly complete terrace

against the building. "To create this appearance," Lopes explained, "we buried the surface of the moat underneath the landscaping. During a seismic event, the concrete moat covers will free themselves. Styrofoam panels and landscape materials will 'pop out,' giving the building the 'breathing space' it needs to properly absorb the horizontal seismic movements. It will look like the edges of the building have sustained damage, but it will only be a few dislodged Styrofoam panels and stone pavers. The building will be fit for occupancy."

BUILDING STRUCTURE

The design called for sweeping views from the main building entrance into the Fern Court and into Wilsey Court. A 200-foot-long double-height glass wall borders this enormous space, limiting opportunity for structural columns. "We had to be creative with our structure," said Lopes. "We worked with the structural engineers to design multi-story trusses to eliminate the need for columns and provide uninterrupted views."

The de Young enclosed in scaffolding in 2003, as the copper panels are being attached to the facade

To put it another way, "making it all go away" is how Lopes describes his firm's role. They had to figure out how to conceal all the structural and functional elements that might compromise the integrity of the design, which called for, among other things, deep interior vistas and generous use of interior glass. Vast wall and ceiling surfaces were intended to be pristine, unblemished by visually distracting utilitarian elements, such as return air grilles and access panels. "In lieu of traditional access panels, we literally created little cities inside hidden shafts, with multilevel steel platforms connected only by vertical ladders." Lopes said, "It is fair to say that conventional strategies to access utilities would not have worked, and we had to come up with our own, often very complex, solutions."

THE ROOF

In a conventional building, the roof is where large mechanical units are located. This would not have been aesthetically acceptable at the new de Young, however, where the roof—visible from the tower—functions as the "fifth facade." The undulating copper roof has a striking composition of ribs and skylights that is integral to the overall design concept. "With the ribs bending in and out and the slices revealing the courtyards, this is where you really see the dynamism of the design," explained Jayne Barlow of Herzog & de Meuron. "When you look down from the tower, you perceive the way the park presses in on the building." The same viewer might also wonder how rainwater runs off and where the exhaust ducts and mechanical units are. Fong & Chan Architects had to accommodate most of the mechanicals inside the building, but they were able to incorporate certain functional elements, such as gutters, into design features of the roof. Exhaust ducts from the conservation laboratory, which by code are required to extend ten feet above adjacent roof

surfaces, were sheathed in a ten-by-forty-foot copper fin that accentuates the pattern of ribs, which conceal the gutters, running the length of the roof. "All other exhaust ducts were hidden in the facade behind perforated copper panels, or in the roof behind perforated cooper ribs," explains Lopes.

THE TOWER

A tour de force of structural ingenuity is the museum's signature nine-story twisted tower. In reality, the tower stretches into a parallelogram as it rises, creating the illusion of twisting. The challenge was to maximize the useable area while still providing significant views out over the city.

"The design team decided to move the required enclosed pressurized exit stairs from the core out to the edge of the tower and open them to the exterior," Lopes explained. This was a truly unique solution that was only possible because of the firm's ability to negotiate life-safety codes with city agencies. "Fong & Chan Architects demonstrated to the Fire Department that a passive open-air stair configuration provided a level of protection equivalent to the prescribed pressurized interior stair enclosure," Lopes said.

The de Young tower is the only recently constructed high-rise building in San Francisco with an exterior exit stair. The design benefits are striking: The zigzag stairs at the ends of the tower, which are open to the air but enclosed in perforated copper panels, are intriguing to behold.

"We knew the people of San Francisco expected a world-class museum," commented Chiu Lin Tse-Chan. "And we were committed in our efforts to deliver a building that exceeded their expectations."

Top left: The foundation being prepared for installation of the base isolation system, with concrete pedestals for the rubber bearings in place

Bottom: View east over the entry court, with the auditorium visible at the first level

Top right: Rubber bearings (in blue), sitting on concrete pedestals, support the vertical steel columns of the building's frame. Bearings allow the structure to slide in the event of an earthquake. Rebar protruding from the foundation (rear) reinforces the base of the tower.

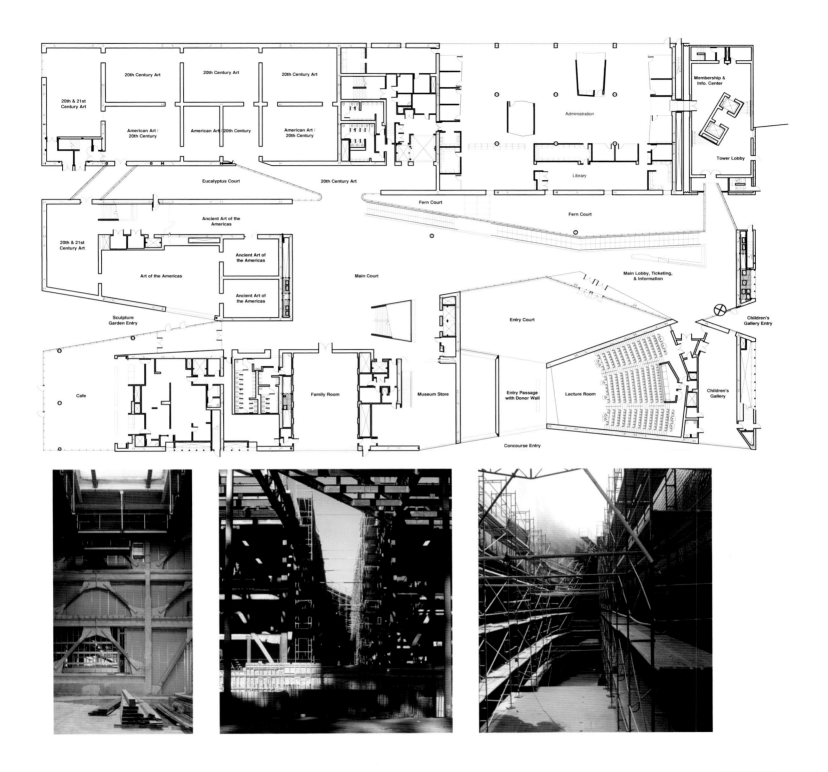

Top: Plan of the first level

Above left: One of the double-height galleries for twentieth-century art
Center: Eucalyptus Court under construction, viewed from the west
Right: Fern Court, viewed from the east

CONSTRUCTING THE DE YOUNG

Left: View east from the art of Oceania wing along the angled front elevation. The framing for the sunshade that extends across the second-story windows is visible at right.

Right: View west of the entry court

Wilsey Court under construction, with the diamond-shaped framing
of the entry court visible to the east

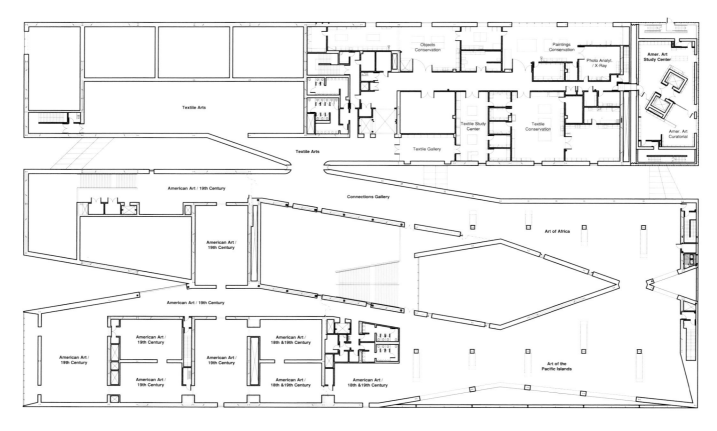

Top: Plan of the second level

Above left: The light box over one of the galleries of American art, surrounded by catwalks for maintenance

Above right: Wilsey Court, with its staircase. Full-height trusses span the space, leaving the court free of columns.

Top: The art of Oceania wing is on the second level, above the double-height auditorium.

Above: The entry court, on the first level. At left is the upper level of the auditorium, with the art of Oceania wing above.

CONSTRUCTING THE DE YOUNG

Above: A detail of the steel framing

Right: The art of Oceania wing before installation of the protective
copper screen over the windows

The corridor leading to the textile gallery, showing the installation
of glass panels surrounding the Eucalyptus Court

Ducts above Wilsey Court curve to fit between the catwalks used
by maintenance staff.

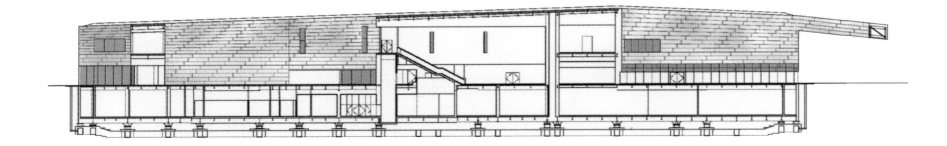

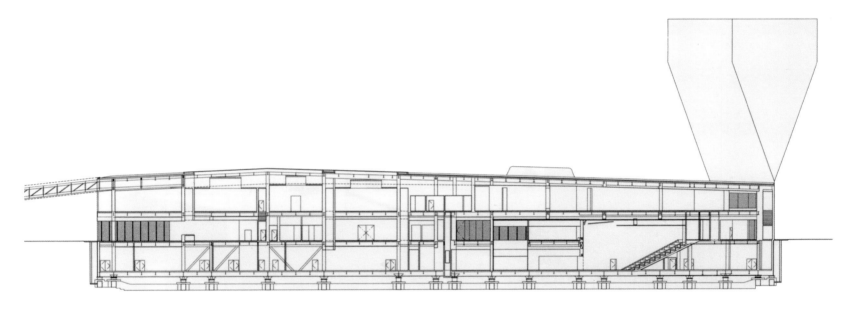

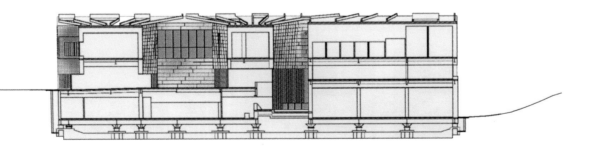

Opposite above: Longitudinal section, north to south
Opposite below: View from the north of the canopy under construction

Top left: View from the west of the canopy under construction, showing the west entrance, the cafe at the lower right, and the loggia at the second level

Top right: View from the southwest
Center: Longitudinal section, south to north
Bottom: Cross section, looking west

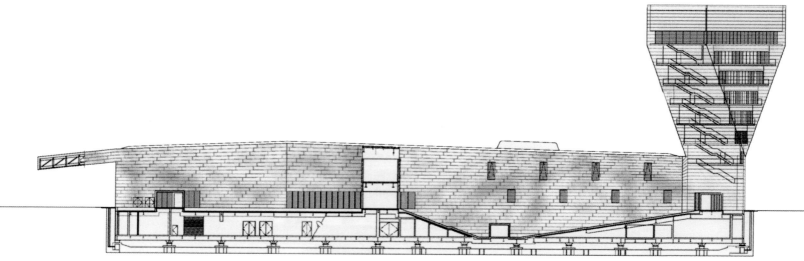

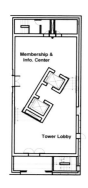

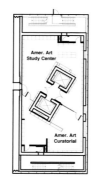

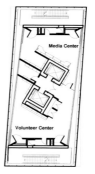

Top: The tower under construction in 2004, showing the topped-off observation deck on the ninth floor

Center: Longitudinal section/elevation, looking north

Across bottom: Tower floor plans, first to ninth floors. The west side of the top floor is parallel to the Pacific Ocean.

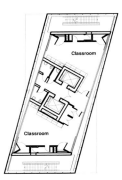

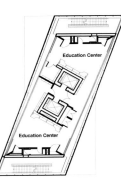

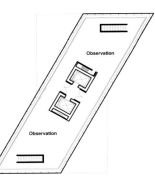

Top: The tower prior to the installation of the copper cladding, showing the exterior fire stairs at the north and south ends and the framing of steel tubes that will support the copper panels

The tower under construction. Steel tubes are attached to each
concrete floor slab by metal brackets.

Perforated copper panels are attached to the steel tubes
by bronze clips.

The roof, the museum's "fifth facade," under construction in 2005.
The view west shows the openings over interior courtyards, the
gallery skylights, the ribs disguising the drainage system, and the
"fin" (center foreground) containing mechanical functions.

Front facade, showing the main entrance and the copper sun shade
across the windows of the art of Oceania wing on the second level

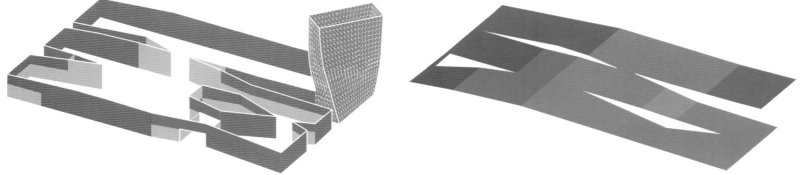

Top: Dimpled and perforated copper facade panels after installation in 2004

Above: Analytical models of the building showing the relation of copper to glass

The copper cladding above the east entrance in 2004

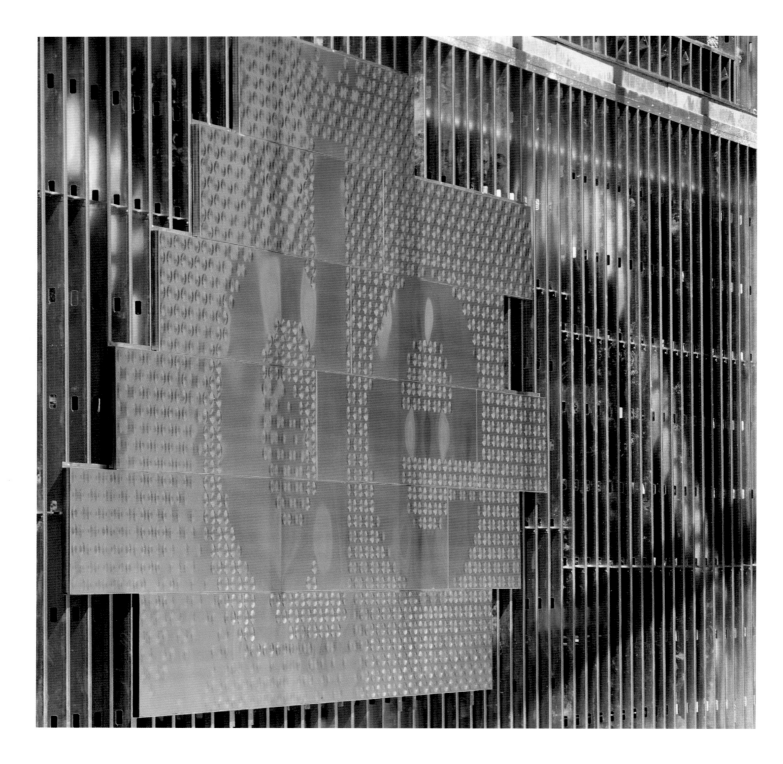

CONSTRUCTING THE DE YOUNG

A mock-up of panels embossed with the ¨de¨ of de Young

Opposite: Newly installed panels at the entrance bearing the name of the museum

Overleaf: The de Young under construction in 2004. View looking north over Golden Gate Park, with the city's Richmond district, San Francisco Bay, and the Marin Headlands beyond

05

INTERVIEW WITH WALTER HOOD

Diana Ketcham

Walter Hood, a specialist in the history of the American urban landscape, was chosen as landscape architect for the new de Young in 2000. His firm, Hood Design, was founded in 1992 and is located in Oakland, California. At the time of his commission, Hood held the chair of the Department of Landscape Architecture and Environmental Planning at the University of California at Berkeley, where he has taught since 1990. His practice is noteworthy for its emphasis on public projects and community design.

DIANA KETCHAM: What are the most valuable results your work can achieve at the new de Young?

WALTER HOOD: It may seem like an odd analogy, but I think of Le Nôtre's garden at the château of Vaux-le-Vicomte, the way that garden harnesses your perception and experience of the entire place, both as you approach it from afar and in the smallest detail. Even as you move away from the château, it is always with you. I want people to experience the new de Young that way—as a building that

Landscape design for the north elevation, with existing stands
of Monterey cypress to the east

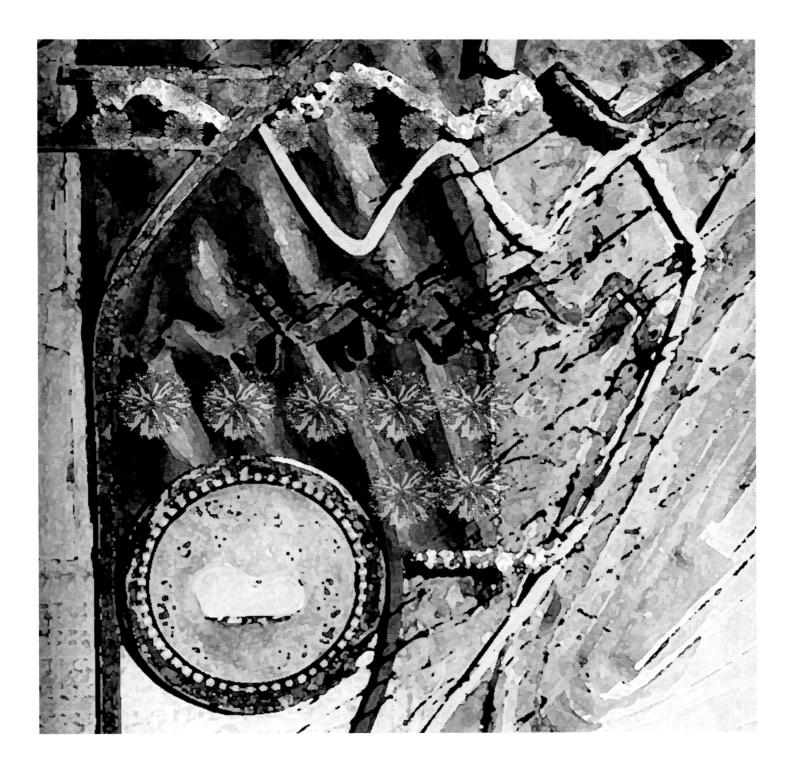

Watercolor sketch by Walter Hood showing the redesigned Pool of
Enchantment and surrounding plantings

property line

Loading
Dock

Cooling
Tower

Electrica

Hillock

Eucalyptus
Forecourt

Eucalyptus Court

Barbro
Osher
Sculpture
Garden

Cafe Access

Cafe Terrace

New de
Young
Museum

property line

Bus Drop-Off

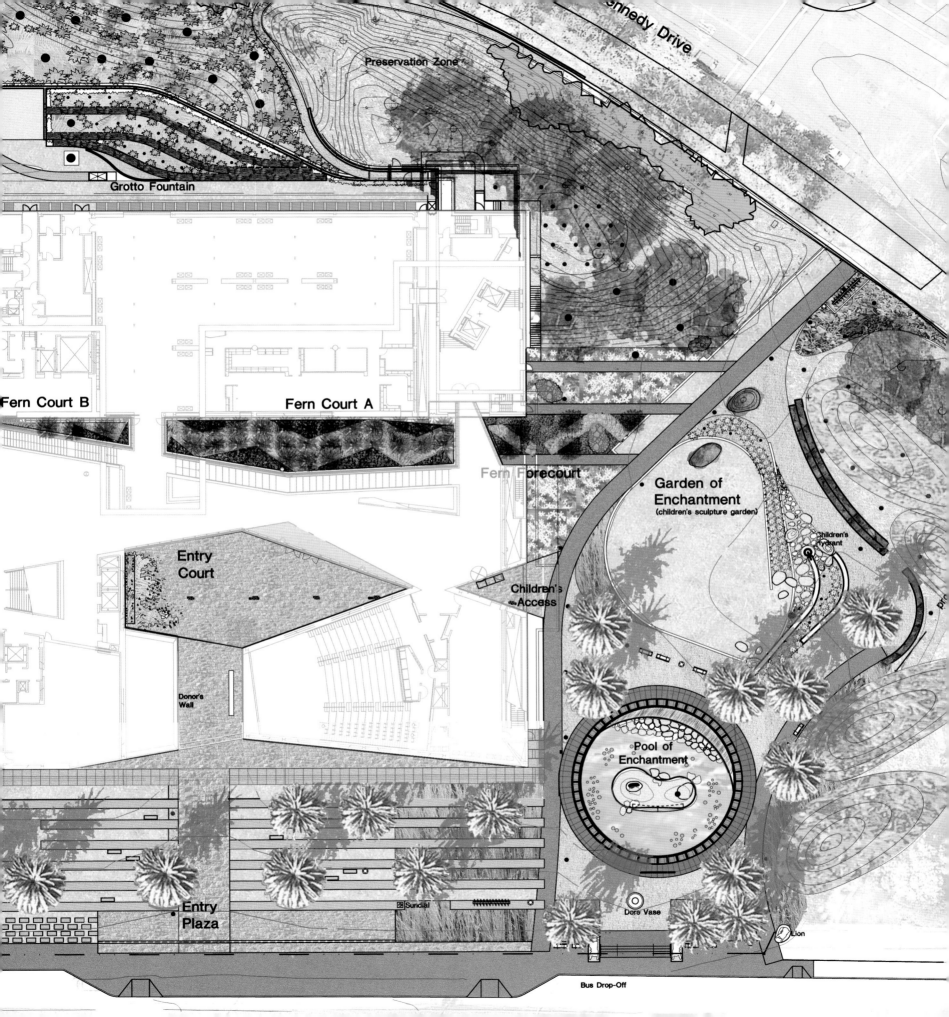

Preservation Zone

Grotto Fountain

Fern Court B

Fern Court A

Fern Forecourt

Garden of
Enchantment
(children's sculpture garden)

Children's
hydrant

Entry
Court

Children's
Access

Donor's
Wall

Pool of
Enchantment

Entry
Plaza

Sundial

Doro Vase

Lion

Bus Drop-Off

has a presence, both up close and from a distance. Our first sketch was all about the site and the locale. We ask: when should people feel they are in a big space, in a small space? We work in an improvisational way, developing physical spaces, then changing their characteristics.

DK: That's setting a high standard. Will the de Young landscape have the heroic feeling of being created by a historic form-giver like Le Nôtre?

WH: Not at all. When the work is finished, I hope that visitors will feel that the landscape around the new museum has always been there, that it is a perfect fit. In landscape architecture there is the magic moment

when the hand of the designer disappears and the environment is just one more part of the experience.

DK: Of course, in a sense Golden Gate Park has "always been there." When the museum was built on this spot in 1894, the Olmsted-inspired park had already existed for twenty years. In what ways did you connect your work to what was already there in Golden Gate Park, or in San Francisco? What special features of the site were you conscious of working with?

WH: We begin with the ground. Here in the park, this is characterized by the sand dunes that the park was built upon. If you can visually and physically experience the

Top: Section of the western end of the site, showing the Barbro Osher Sculpture Garden and the Eucalyptus Court

Bottom: The cafe terrace under the cantilever, overlooking the sculpture garden

ground and its material, you realize that Golden Gate Park is a re-creation of nature through human interventions. An entirely new flora and fauna has been introduced over the 150 years that human beings have developed this ground.

DK: You are reminding us that the park was an artifice from the very beginning. Does that mean your selection of plants and forms is unrelated to what most people think of as the natural environment surrounding the museum?

WH: No, the geology and history of the park are a given. Our plan literally emerged from looking at the park's grading plan, historically and contemporarily. The contouring in many places mimics the dune geography, and we decided to build upon this ground plane expression. We were also interested in the earlier introduction of particular plants to this ecology, i.e. palms, cypress, redwoods, tree ferns, to name a few. In the sculpture garden, we are creating a remnant landform, a five- to six-foot hillock of sand that is planted with native grasses. Formally, the hillock blurs the distant landscape with the near and brings the landscape scale down to the ground at the cafe terrace. The landform recalls the historic ground. On the other side of the building, in the Children's Garden, the ground is sculpted, articulating another contouring pattern associated with dunes. Throughout the design the ground is articulated with pattern, utilizing paving, planting, and contouring. Inside the building, the courtyards recapitulate the park's natural history. As you move from one courtyard to another, we have conceptualized the travels of sand in from the Pacific, west to east. It is transformed into gravel, then stones, and, finally, into large boulders in the Children's Garden. You will experience the idea of grand movement through this progression.

DK: You mentioned the flora planted by previous park designers. Haven't you rehabilitated the reputations of some examples of flora that had fallen out of fashion, or worse, been categorized as environmentally or politically incorrect? What about the poor, maligned eucalyptus?

WH: We are using eucalyptus trees as specimen trees, as they were once employed in the park's design and throughout northern California. Instead of planting them in windrows or masses and clumps, as they appear elsewhere in the park, they'll be contained, cut back, and grown as shrub mass. Their aroma and leaf mulch will transform the courtyard. Giant tree ferns will be planted in the sloping courtyard. You will see them as you move from the basement up to the second floor. They recall the groves of tree ferns near the museum, but here in the museum court they are formalized.

DK: What you have in Golden Gate Park is not just one site, but a complex of different environments that come together at the museum. This is where the classical Concourse meets the Japanese Tea Garden, both of which were part of the original 1894 layout for the Midwinter International Exposition, which gave birth to the museum. Then there are the naturalistic plantings along John F. Kennedy Drive, which are much more prominent now that the Asian Art Museum has been demolished. The clearing away of those buildings has opened up and highlighted this part of the park in many ways. It gives us a view of the Japanese Tea Garden that is new and very beautiful.

WH: We kept asking ourselves how we could bring the park right up so it was pushing against the building, reinforcing the plantings along the drive with more of the existing redwoods, cypress, and pines.

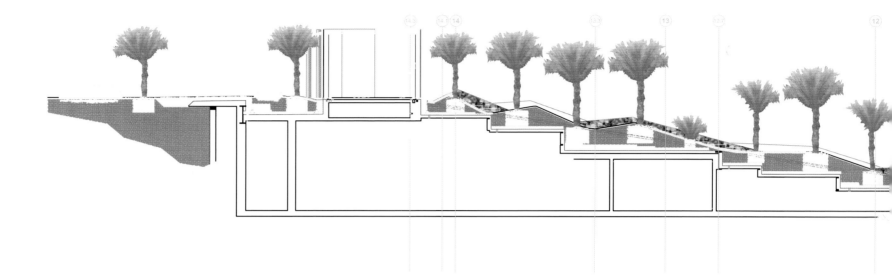

DK: How do you see your work in relation to the design of the architects Herzog & de Meuron?

WH: Our work complements theirs in several ways. We reinforce the building's relationship to the landscape by exploiting the spatial openness. Landscape form passes through the building and connects it to the park. Also, these architects work with surface expression, and we continue this on the ground, where we create a changing and hopefully muted expression. But more frankly, I believe the perfect complement to their work is a quiet expression of form and space. We are trying to create spaces that are nice to be in and that bring you closer to the architecture, the site, and the park.

DK: There were several aspects of the architects' design that were controversial initially. Or, you could say, it was not easy for the public to imagine how they would be realized. The effect of the patterned copper skin on a building of this scale was a question mark in many people's minds. Did the

pattern and color of the copper, or how quickly it would age, enter in to your design decisions?

WH: Yes and no. It is a no-brainer not to try and match the color of copper, even though it is tempting. From the beginning the architects and we ourselves felt the landscape should not try to copy the copper colors directly. Instead we chose to create a set of color values that emanate from the ground surfaces, i.e. the kaleidoscope of colors found in the sand: black, tan, red, green, etc.

DK: Several of the landscapes have specific functions that go beyond the creation of space in the ways you have mentioned: the interface of the cafe terrace, the Osher Sculpture Garden, and the Japanese Tea Garden at the west end of the building must have required a particular strategy from you.

WH: Designing a sculpture garden for us began with thinking about how artworks should be viewed in the landscape—Golden Gate Park. We wanted to create

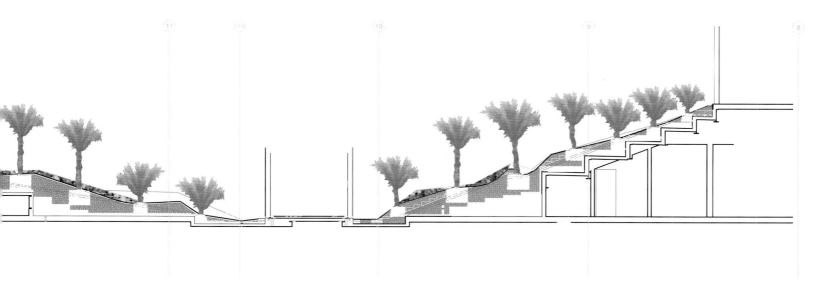

proximity to paths without making a rigid grid, and you want to create pleasurable spaces between views. In the Sculpture Garden we thought carefully about the tree species that provide canopy, materials to spatially define outdoor rooms. Should we have color? What should the scale be? What are the textures? Gingko and maple trees were the answer. They are big and they both provide intense color—from light green to gold and red in the fall. They are both deciduous, and the gingkos provide a little of the idiosyncratic—they are a new plant to the concourse landscape. I like that! Both trees have an Eastern origin, and the maples exist in the Japanese Tea Garden, which meets western edge of the Sculpture Garden.

DK: What about the paths you mentioned?

WH: All the paving in the gardens is sandy to black in color. This creates a muted backdrop and highlights the sand ground plane. The stone we chose picks up the changing spectrum of colors in the copper. We decided that pathways that connect the museum to the park should be consistent with the large-scale park circulation pattern, so we used asphalt. Other ground surfaces are allowed to reinforce spaces around the museum.

DK: Early on in the design process, the press described you as a "foil" to Herzog & de Meuron. It was as if landscaping could "warm up" what some mistakenly feared might be an uninvitingly cold or "tough" building. What were the qualities that you saw in Herzog & de Meuron's work when you visited it in Switzerland?

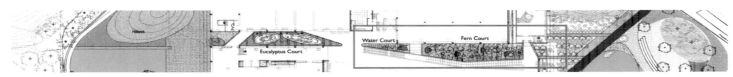

Top: Section of the Fern Court
Above: Site plan showing the Fern Court

WH: First, I never saw their buildings as cold or tough. Their interest to me has always been linked to the ephemeral nature of the material. What others see as cold and tough, they see as light, air, pattern, surface, and color. The transformation of the material experientially and physically in their work is exciting. Their ethic of examiming all sides of things really fascinates me, also, particularly their way of showing how simple form and materials can have other attributes that are not readily visible in a drawing or model.

DK: At one stage you were in daily contact with the architects. How would you describe your working relationship with Herzog & de Meuron?

WH: Our working relationship is dynamic. We met frequently to discuss concepts and approaches to the landscape and its interface with the building. Part of a successful collaboration is the willingness of participants to listen to other views and attitudes. I believe we were both open during this conversation, and the benefits can be seen in the results, from the basic formal plan, to the selection of plants and the ground surface, to the coordination of the finishes.

Top and opposite:The Garden of Enchantment, with the sphinxes, the Doré vase, and palm trees repositioned from the former site. The Pool of Enchantment was rebuilt as a round pool containing the original Earl Cummings sculptures.

DK: What are some of the specific features of the architecture that you considered in your design? The stated concept of the architects from the very beginning was to "bring the park into the building."

WH: We kept asking ourselves, how much can we push the park up against the museum? We filled the courtyards with eucalyptus and giant ferns, creating large-scale terrariums.

DK: What about the elements from the old museum? It appears that you as the landscape architect were given the responsibility for preserving these architectural remnants, instead of the architects, who did not keep the Hearst Court, for example, which had been requested by some citizens' groups. The symbolic ties with the past—the pair of sphinxes from the 1894 Egyptian Revival Fine Arts Building; the Pool of Enchantment, a survivor from the Mullgardt building—these are in your territory, are they not? How did you decide to use them in the Children's Garden, which you have named the Garden of Enchantment?

WH: We couldn't duplicate or move the old pool because it was part of the entry sequence of the building. We placed the new pool at the entry to the Children's Garden. We made the pool circular, which allows you to move around it unfettered. The design of the new de Young landscape is intended to encourage a more diverse audience to use the museum and the park. We have created two new gardens, the Children's Garden and the Osher Sculpture Garden, which are easy to access and will be new destinations in the city and in the park. As visitors enjoy these new amenities, we hope they will venture into the museum, appreciate the great collection, and experience what I believe will be one of the city's landmark buildings.

On 11 March 2005 Jacques Herzog, founding partner, with Pierre de Meuron, of the Herzog & de Meuron architecture firm, met with Aaron Betsky, director of the Netherlands Architecture Institute in Rotterdam. The two spoke at the designers' sprawling Basel complex of renovated houses and sheds along the Rhine River. They discussed the fortuitous meeting between museum officials and the architects that led to the de Young commission, Herzog's response to the museum's site in Golden Gate Park, his desire to break through the rigid frameworks that usually contain art museums, and the architectural uses of fog.

AARON BETSKY: How did you get the commission for the de Young and why did you accept it?

JACQUES HERZOG: This was quite a unique start: one day Dede Wilsey and Harry Parker just dropped in our office. They were on a tour of several buildings—they stopped in Basel to visit the Beyeler Foundation designed by Renzo Piano—and once in Basel they thought that they wanted to talk to us, and that's how we got in touch. It was a very spontaneous meeting because they didn't let us know they were coming, and it was unprepared on both sides. It was more about getting to know each other and testing whether we would respond to what their needs would be. It was

a very positive contact. To do a new home for the museum's comprehensive collection of ethnographic art sounded quite interesting.

AB: What was so interesting about ethnographic art?

JH: We have a very good museum of that kind of art in Basel, but I find the way it is presented not very interesting. There, like in most American museums, the selected pieces are individually highlighted, and they look more like objects in a jewelry store than those in a museum. We thought the art should be less hierarchically presented—more like contemporary art than like bijoux. We spoke about new forms of presentation very early in the process and, of course, about the striking setting of the museum in Golden Gate Park.

AB: You knew the site because of your work on the Dominus Winery in Napa Valley?

JH: We didn't know the institution very well but we knew the site. To do a major public building in this park was quite a challenge for everybody and quite a thrill. We were just finishing the Dominus Winery, and we were also working on the Kramlich house in Napa Valley. So the

museum project was a chance to create a cluster of different projects, which is always very interesting because you can then test totally different approaches to architecture.

AB: Why is that diversity so important?

JH: For different reasons. One is because the clients and the sites and the programs are so different. But the diversity of approach is also a method or a tool to escape your own routine.

AB: Please elaborate on this notion of making a non-hierarchical museum, and why that is appropriate for museums in general and for this museum in this location in particular.

JH: The hierarchy in museums is a leftover from an elitist way of thinking in which the superiority of our culture over that of the "other" should be demonstrated. Also, within our specific culture a priori positioning was more widespread than open access to the differences of forms and the thinking behind them. San Francisco, which as a city is so much about diversity of different cultures and cultural influences, should have a new de Young museum that is open to experimental and non-hierarchical presentations of its holdings.

AB: The mechanism that you used to achieve this breakdown of hierarchy has a lot to do with breaking traditions, as much as building on them, which is to take all the elements of the classical museum and mix them up, rearrange them. Is that correct?

JH: We tried to do this mostly with the galleries. There are classical galleries for American painting, sculpture, and decorative arts of the seventeenth century to the nineteenth century that are very intimate, almost in the tradition of private homes, for which the objects were originally conceived. These galleries contrast with very fluid gallery spaces, organized in a kind of *plan libre* layout, where we introduced the oversized wood frames and vitrines, which are ideal for presenting the collections of Oceanic and African art. These vitrines are like large windows, something halfway between architecture and interior design. They connect the inside with the outside. The same happens with the garden wedges cutting into the building. They can be seen as vitrines filled with nature displayed inside the building, but, in fact, they are nothing but enclosed space arranged in an unexpected way. In other words: one of our de Young strategies was to use the familiar and face it with the unfamiliar. Using the familiar—for example, in the shape and fit out of the American galleries—was not for the sake of quoting it, nor is it an intellectual joke. We simply use existing and familiar forms and qualities wherever it makes sense, or whenever nothing better is available or nothing better comes to our mind. There is still always a lot to invent and reinvent, such as the above-mentioned vitrines for the more "fluid" gallery sequences or the embossed copper cladding for the facade and the twisting tower. This pragmatic combination of things seems very natural to us.

AB: But it goes beyond the galleries, this breaking down?

JH: Yes, of course. It involves every part of the building. Here at the de Young the most significant example is the way people move through the spaces and experience landscape and art.

AB: The landscape and the building, inside and outside, mix together?

JH: I mentioned the vitrines and the garden wedges, which are also a kind of vitrines. Another key element for this blur of inside and outside is the large perforated canopy that opens up to the Japanese garden. The Japanese garden thus becomes part of the museum displays in some way. The park, the artwork, and the viewer are involved and bound in a process of looking and being looked at: the viewer becoming aware of the work of art, becoming aware of himself or herself, and becoming aware of his or her presence here and now. This sounds stupidly simple, but, in fact, it is what we always thought a museum space should really achieve. Here we tried to come as close as we could to this ideal perceptional condition, which was a real challenge because of the diversity of the gallery types.

AB: There also seems to be some interest in making large public spaces that are not hierarchical.

JH: They are not hierarchical because they are part of a network of topographical fix points found all through the building: the grand stair, Wilsey Court, the intersections of the different galleries, the educational tower, the platform—they are all like topographical points where one can meet. You can describe them easily or even name them and say, "let's meet there," and people will immediately know what you're talking about. Wilsey Court, with the huge mural that Gerhard Richter has developed specifically for that space, has an outstanding, almost central position within the whole building. It is the modern-day version of the Hearst Court, which was so key in the previous building.

AB: But most of the spaces are not arranged in the standard sequence that one might expect.

JH: Exactly. Our concept of topographical fix points replaces the hierarchical museum concept that goes back to the Beaux-Arts tradition, but it maintains and reinterprets some of these traditional elements, which have proved to still work well.

AB: The de Young as a building is rather monolithic, though. Was that the intention, or did you want it originally to be more part of the landscape?

JH: You perceive it as monolithic?

AB: Yes, it does seem rather monolithic, of a piece, much more coherent as an object than I would have expected.

JH: We see it as coherent rather than monolithic. It was very important for us to conceive it as one thing that integrates all the collections and therefore all the cultural diversity expressed through them. Had we gone for something fragmented, like the pavilion concept that we originally developed on our boards, we would have introduced a notion of segregation and separation. We clearly wanted to avoid that as much as the above-mentioned hierarchies. Despite its coherence, the building integrates the outside: the landscaped nature of the park and even the whole city.

AB: But the exterior also was a way of making a coherent building in that natural setting. You talked about it adapting itself to the flow of the landscape. It also is a building that responds to the flow of the topography of the park.

JH: The museum is almost built on sand dunes. We wanted the building to reflect this almost literally. We wanted very much to keep the existing sand that was exposed by the construction site in the garden area around the building, and even bring it in through the various wedges and canyonlike spaces that cut into the volume of the building. Instead of sand we used plants, which refer to the park's vegetation. Those planted wedges can be seen as sloped vitrines. They integrate well with the concept of the network of topographical fix points.

AB: You have talked about wanting to make a building that was not a metaphor because you don't work with metaphors, but one that somehow evoked the climate and the park and the nature of the institution. If it is not a metaphor how does it do that, how does it achieve that evocation?

JH: That is a very important point not only for this project. Avoiding the metaphor means that you as an architect don't tell a story about how something should be seen or read or understood but that you expose people to their own mental and physical experience. The building really does work like topography. You walk up and down. You are faced with nature. Nature really "walks" into the building. And you can also go and breathe the air. All of that is not an illustration or an illusion or a representation of something, but it is what it is. That is also very important when it comes to art and the perception of art because otherwise you could as well learn about—let's say Gerhard Richter—just based on a magazine with pictures. You can identify a lot of details in the printed version of an artwork but you never get the real color, the real size, the real proportions. You're never really faced one-to-one with the artwork itself. And the building should allow you to do that. And even more: the building should stress that moment of the real encounter. This has always been a fact, and it has become even more crucial today in a world dominated by digital information technology. It's the only true asset left for architecture.

AB: Is there a difference in how you design a museum, something that is supposed to have a general cultural meaning and that perhaps should be larger or stranger or just other than daily life, and something for the marketplace?

JH: Marketplace and "general cultural meaning" don't necessarily exclude one another, do they? Every great museum builds its own marketplace around which it gathers a growing community of patrons, donors, and supporters of all generations. Without this social network museums wouldn't survive; they would simply not work not only because of lacking money but also because of lacking life. A museum is a kind of cultural marketplace. American museums especially have a tradition of privately or half privately organized communities that support them, whereas in Europe the state has traditionally taken that role. Today many European museums are in deep trouble because of the state's almost empty pockets and the lack of community willing and trained to fill out that role.

AB: How did you try to encourage that sense of community at the de Young?

JH: It was already very strongly implemented. They had a powerful and committed leader, Dede Wilsey, who was the strong woman behind the whole process. Not only because she gave so much money but because she invested an incredible amount of energy. We were very impressed by the kind of pioneering role she played when it came to discussing and defending unconventional solutions that we put on the table. She motivated and encouraged people who couldn't have been more diverse. You as a museum person will know what I'm talking about. There is always so much resistance around, so much energy needed to convince people to take the newer and riskier way and even more to pay for it. That's a huge and inevitable task in every project of this scale and importance. Such a project needs clear leadership by someone on the client's side, otherwise it will fail. Here Mrs. Wilsey took that leadership and was very helpful in the process of maintaining the enthusiasm within the museum community.

AB: So did you encourage community by making the outdoor cafe, by making the tower—how do the elements in your design attempt to do that?

JH: The building very logically reflects the social structure of its patrons and supporters. Besides the core functions of the museum—the exhibition, storage, and maintenance of the collections—the building offers a series of platforms for the community to meet. The cafe is much more than a traditional museum cafe, it is a great event place. The auditorium, Wilsey Court, the grand stair, the educational tower—they all can be seen and used by people in various ways. Many of these social platforms that you find in American museums—take the Walker Art Center, whose expansion project we opened earlier this year, as another example—don't exist in European museums, which are traditionally more hermetic, more like classical treasure chests.

AB: And the tower, for instance, is meant to establish an identity, right?

JH: The tower does several things. It connects the museum, which is integrated in the park, with the rest of the city. The tower's twisting shape describes the geometrical shift from the off-axis position of its base to the alignment of its top with the rectangular shape of the park and the street grid of the city. It contains the educational facilities of the museum and offers a viewing platform with a gorgeous view of the whole Bay Area. The old building had a tower;

the new, twisting tower can also be seen as its contemporary version and as its follower as an icon for San Francisco.

AB: How did you see your role as an architect in relationship to that of the curators?

JH: We spoke with the curators very early in the process. Exhibiting, presenting, looking inside out and outside in were key ideas for both the architectural and curatorial concepts of the building. Of course we wish we could have gone further and exhibited things even less hierarchically, exhibit them more provocatively—for example, like merchandise in a supermarket or on shelves in archeological storage. Our idea behind the installation display and the gallery display was always to provide the best possible conditions for a fresh encounter between artwork and visitor. The building offers a rich variety of gallery types so that the curators will be able to change and rearrange the way the collections are presented over the years. This change is necessary for the institution to renew itself and to rethink and reinvent many possible ways artworks can be perceived and understood.

AB: For all that, there is a grand staircase, a *piano nobile*, and there is a cafe with the smell of coffee. It still does have a lot of the traditional elements of a museum building. Do you wish that it had fewer of those elements or were you exactly trying to use them?

JH: As I said before we love using traditional elements whenever they make sense. If not, we try to find something new. The one thing we really hate but were not able to avoid is the smell of coffee, which is so typical in American interior spaces. As soon as you enter the country through immigration, you are trapped in this inevitable smell of coffee, which penetrates rugs, hung ceilings, curtains, and clothes.

AB: You seem obsessed with the smell.

JH: I really dislike smell in public spaces when it is so all over, like the smell of bad coffee in American interiors. We should try to find an olfactory weapon to neutralize it. The olfactory world is clearly as important as the audiovisual world but strangely fewer and fewer people seem to respond to it with consciousness, even though it conditions our perception and steers our behavior.

AB: It seems to me that the bigger problem is actually noise in public spaces rather than smell.

JH: Do you mean in museums or in cities in general?

AB: In cities but also in museums.

JH: Sound pollution from video installations spilling out to other galleries and parts of the museum can be very awkward. The sound of people, kids, or classes doesn't bother us at all. Sound seems to be more individual and different in each museum and less of an uninterrupted torture like bad smell.

AB: You talked with great enthusiasm and love of the fog, and how the fog of San Francisco had inspired you, and how you wanted the building to respond to the fog.

JH: The fog has inspired us insofar that we wanted the building to deal with it, to use it as a conscious element of the design. It does so in two ways: first, through the fuzzy, perforated facade panels that seem to blur the edges of the

The view north from the ninth floor of the tower

building volume. Clearly the fog enhances this moment of the blur. Secondly, we chose copper as a material because it ages well. We know how it performs and transforms itself over the years. Copper acts almost like a scientific instrument that measures and expresses the impact and change of the climate. The impact of fog, humidity, and heavy sun are likely to transform the embossed and perforated copper panels much more positively than they would any other facade material.

AB: But you had a sense that you wanted this building to loom up out of the fog or to maybe slide into the fog.

JH: Do you want to say that behind this idea of fog and the responding facade material lies, in fact, a romantic attitude? Perhaps—the romantic understood as an attitude that involves the whole environment: yes. The romantic understood as some kind of tasteful mysticism: no.

AB: But also the emotive quality of that fog, the softness of it, or the fact that it blurs things.

JH: We have used the concept of the blur in many projects for different reasons. One is to express doubt rather than certainty when it comes to defining or positioning volumes in a given context. Here the blur will be enhanced by the fog penetrating through the multiple perforations in the facade panels. It will be especially interesting to see the fog building up in layers, with the lower part of the building hidden in a cloud of fog and the tower twisting out of it, or vice versa.

156 The de Young in Golden Gate Park, with the Marin Headlands in the distance

Overleaf: The museum from the southwest, with the pollarded plane trees of the Music Concourse in the foreground

Previous spread: Views of the tower from the east

Above: The cantilever from the west

Opposite: The cantilever from the north

Above: Detail of the lighting

Opposite: Facade detail
Above: The cantilever from the southwest

Overleaf: The entry court, with Andy Goldsworthy's *Drawn Stone*
(2005). Museum purchase, gift of Lonna and Marshall Wais, 2004.5

Stairs from the lower level to Wilsey Court, with the Fern Court
visible through the glass

Two views of the stairwell linking the first level and the lower level

174   Two views of the main entry

The staircase in Wilsey Court, with the information desk at left

Opposite: The cafe

Above: Overlooking the Fern Court from the entry area

The modern and contemporary art wing on the first level

181

The modern and contemporary art wing on the first level

The American art wing on the second level

The art of Oceania wing on the second level

188   The art of Africa wing on the second level

190   Above: Interior of the tower's south stairs

Opposite: The tower exterior

Overleaf: View of the museum's roof from the south stairs of the
tower, with the Spreckels Temple of Music at left

The north elevation of the building, from John F. Kennedy Drive

Details of the facade and the tower

BUILDING AND CONSTRUCTION INFORMATION

NEW DE YOUNG DESIGN TEAM

Client: Corporation of the Fine Arts
  Museums of San Francisco: the New
  de Young Museum
President of the Board of Trustees: Diane
  B. Wilsey
Director of Museums: Harry S. Parker III
Project Director: Deborah Frieden

Primary Designers: Herzog & de Meuron
  Architekten AG
Basel, Switzerland
Partner in Charge: Pierre de Meuron
Project Architect: Ascan Mergenthaler
Project Manager: Mark Loughnan

Principal Architect: Fong & Chan Architects
San Francisco, California
Principals: Chiu Lin Tse-Chan and
  David Fong
Project Manager: Nuno Lopes

Landscape Architect: Hood Design
Oakland, California
Principal: Walter Hood

General Contractor: Swinerton Builders
San Francisco, California

Structural, Civil, and Geotechnical Engineers:
Rutherford & Chekene
San Francisco, California

Facade Contractor: A. Zahner Company
Kansas City, Missouri
Partner in Charge: L. William Zahner

Mechanical, Electrical, and Plumbing:
Ove Arup Group and Partners, California

Lighting Design: Ove Arup Group and
Partners, London

THE NEW DE YOUNG

Location: 50 Hagiwara Tea Garden Drive,
Golden Gate Park, San Francisco, California

Opening: October 15, 2005
Groundbreaking: June 2002

Construction budget: $135 million
Total budget: $202 million

Building size: Two stories above grade, one
story below, with a nine-story, 144-foot tower

Total floorplate: 240 feet wide, 420 feet long
Total interior area: 293,000 square feet
(Double the size of the previous de Young,
on a smaller footprint)

Exhibition areas: 84,000 square feet
(More than double the previous
exhibition space)

Education areas: 20,000 square feet

Conservation facilities: 13,000 square feet

Barbro Osher Sculpture Garden and Terrace:
35,000 square feet

George and Judy Marcus Children's Garden
(The Garden of Enchantment):
47,000 square feet

Nancy B. and Jake Hamon Education Tower,
observation floor: 2,500 square feet

Structure:
5,122 tons of structural steel
1,500 tons of concrete
2,500 tons of rebar

Facade:
7,200 unique panels, with 1,500,000
  embossings
950,000 pounds of copper (more than 50%
  recycled)
300,000 pounds of glass
70,000 pounds of architectural bronze

Foundation:
Base isolation system

The tower at night

ENDNOTES

CHAPTER 1

A longer version of this article, "M. H. de Young Memorial Museum," is available at the San Francisco Public Library History Center.

1. Cynthia Stretch, "Chronological List of Changes to the M. H. de Young Memorial Museum," prepared for the Archives of the Fine Arts Museums of San Francisco, 28 August 1987. The museum was legally turned over by the parks commissioners on 23 March 1895, which was long celebrated as Founder's Day.

2. *San Francisco Chronicle*, 15 August 1893, 10.

3. A. Page Brown (1859–1896), who previously worked for McKim, Mead & White, was one of the leading architects in San Francisco in the 1890s. He designed the California building at the 1893 World's Columbian Exposition in Chicago and the Ferry Building in San Francisco.

4. *California Midwinter International Exposition Guide and Souvenir* (San Francisco: Whitcher, Allen & Boldemann, [1894]), n.p. See also Arthur Chandler and Marvin Nathan, *The Fantastic Fair* (St. Paul: Pogo Press, 1993).

5. Charles C. McDougall (1857–1930) was a San Francisco architect who was in practice with his father, Barnett McDougall, as McDougall & Son (1879–1897); the firm designed dwellings, the Children's Hospital, the Church of Christ, and the California Bible Society. Later he practiced with his younger brothers, Benjamin and George, as McDougall Brothers (1896–1913) in San Francisco, Bakersfield, and Fresno.

6. *San Francisco Chronicle*, 31 December 1893, entire issue.

7. *San Francisco Chronicle*, 17 July 1893, 2; 18 July 1893, 8. See also Terence Young, *Building San Francisco's Parks, 1850–1930* (Baltimore: Johns Hopkins University Press, 2004), 147. Young is a geographer teaching at California State Polytechnic University, Pomona.

8. Edwards Roberts, "Some Architectural Effects," *Overland Monthly*, Midwinter Fair Number, 23, no. 136 (April 1894): 349.

9. Young, *Building San Francisco's Parks*, 155.

10. Executive Committee of the California Midwinter International Exposition, *Guide to the Halls and Galleries of the Memorial Museum* (San Francisco: Crocker Company, 1895), 47.

11. Roberts, "Some Architectural Effects," 350.

12. Young, *Building San Francisco's Parks*, 147. In fact, a small museum already existed in the park in the Sharon Building at the Children's Playground.

13. Executive Committee, *Guide to the Halls and Galleries of the Memorial Museum*, 9.

14. Marjorie C. Driscoll, *The M. H. de Young Memorial Museum* (San Francisco: The Park Commission, 1921), 12.

15. Pamela Forbes, ed., *100 Years in Golden Gate Park: A Pictorial History of the M. H. de Young Memorial Museum* (San Francisco: The Fine Arts Museums, 1995), 7–8; Driscoll, *The M. H. de Young Memorial Museum*, passim; Christopher Pollock, *Golden Gate Park* (San Francisco: Arcadia Publishing, 2003), 29–41. While from the perspective of a twenty-first-century art museum, the early collection as a whole may have deserved the anonymous disparaging characterization as "the city's attic," de Young and his early curators did not purport to have established an art museum. Their intention was to create a municipal museum that would attract and educate the general public. Elements of this early collection deserved respect in a variety of areas: art, California history, natural history, and California Indians.

16. Charles Presby Wilcomb was curator of the Memorial Museum from its opening until 1905. In 1909 he became the first curator of the Oakland Museum. See "Oakland Museum Curator is Dead," *San Francisco Chronicle*, 24 June 1915; "Mute Witness to Vanished Cultures: Wilcomb's Indian Collections." *Museum of California* 3, no. 7 (January 1980): 4. John W. Rogers (1842–1930) was employed in the insurance business and a member of the Civil Service Commission when he was made curator on 15 July 1905. Upon his departure on 1 July 1908, he became chief assistant clerk for the Board of Supervisors. See "John W. Rogers, Supervisors' Chief Assistant Aid, Drops Dead at City Hall," *San Francisco Chronicle*, 15 July 1930, 3. Dr. Albert E. Gray served as curator from June 1908 to February 1910. Nothing is known about his training or experience. George Haviland Barron served two terms as curator between 1910 and 1933. He was considered an authority on the early history of the Roman Catholic Church in California. See A. T. Leonard Jr., "In Memoriam: George Haviland Barron, 1869–1942," *California Historical Society Quarterly* 21 (December 1942): 378. William Altman served as curator from 13 April to 1 November 1917 when he died of typhoid fever. Prior to his appointment as curator, Altman had been assistant curator at the Memorial Museum since his hire by Charles P. Wilcomb in 1901. See "Park Museum Curator Goes to Final Rest," *San Francisco Chronicle*, 3 November 1917, 10. Charles E. Penez, who followed Altman, was a civil engineer who had worked for eleven years in the Department of Public Works. The son of an artist, he was described as "an

artist as well as an engineer.... The new curator has long been a private collector. He is versed in numismatics and in the collection and classification of stamps, minerals and curios. Other studies have brought him a knowledge of ornithology and taxidermy." See "New Curator in Charge at Park Museum," *San Francisco Chronicle*, 5 December 1917, 10. Units 1 and 2 were built during Penez's tenure as curator.

17. Quoted in Forbes, *100 Years in Golden Gate Park*, 7.

18. Driscoll, *The M. H. de Young Memorial Museum*, 10.

19. Others include the Brooklyn Museum of Art (1897); the Buffalo and Erie County Historical Society, built as the New York State Building at the Pan American Exposition (1901); the California Palace of the Legion of Honor in San Francisco (1916); the Museum of Fine Arts in Houston (1924); and the Detroit Institute of the Arts (1927).

20. *San Francisco Chronicle*, 24 September 1916, 37.

21. After the de Young addition, Mullgardt became an increasingly marginal figure, whose visionary schemes, such as a bridge for San Francisco Bay with skyscrapers as towers, won him a posthumous fame. See Robert Judson Clark, "Louis Christian Mullgardt and the Court of Ages," *Journal of the Society of Architectural Historians* 21, no. 4 (December 1962): 171–178; Robert Judson Clark, "The Life and Accomplishments of Louis Christian Mullgardt (1866–1942)," master's thesis, Stanford University, 1964; Irving F. Morrow, "Louis Christian Mullgardt, 1866–1942," *Architect and Engineer* 148 (February 1942): 42–43; and Rexford Newcomb, "The Work of Louis Christian Mullgardt in Honolulu," *Western Architect* (November 1922): 123–126.

22. *San Francisco Chronicle*, 15 April 1917, 57. H. J. Brunnier (1882–1971) was a prominent structural engineer in San Francisco from his arrival in 1906. He designed many of the first reinforced concrete structures at the Port of San Francisco, the structural frames of the city's major skyscrapers of the 1920s to the 1930s, and a bridge with the "largest concrete girder span in the world." Bailey Millard, *History of the San Francisco Bay Region* 2 vols. (Chicago: American Historical Society, 1924), 180.

23. *San Francisco Chronicle*, 15 April 1917, 57.

24. *San Francisco Chronicle*, 22 February 1919, 11.

25. Irving F. Morrow, "Memorial Museum, Golden Gate Park, San Francisco," *The Building Review* 17 (August 1919): 26; Willis E. Huson, "The Memorial Museum at Golden Gate Park," *The Western Architect* 27 (December 1918): 8–10; "Memorial Museum, Golden Gate Park, San Francisco, California," *Architectural Review* 12, no. 2 (February 1921): plates 19–20.

26. Newcomb, "Mullgardt in Honolulu," 123.

27. Frona Eunice Wait Colburn, "The Things of Substance in Wishing Land," *Overland Monthly* 87, no. 1 (January 1929): 19.

28. Forbes, *100 Years in Golden Gate Park*, 7, 9.

29. Meyer was one of the best established and most prolific commercial architects in San Francisco from 1906 to the 1950s. He had been involved in planning of the Civic Center and was the architect of many downtown buildings, including several Pacific Gas & Electric substations, the Humboldt Bank, the Monadnock Building, and the Financial Center Building. He often worked with partners. Jorgensen and Keyser, who signed most of the de Young drawings, had worked form him as draftsmen and in this case were elevated to the status of partners.

30. *San Francisco Chronicle*, 1 March 1931, picture section, 5.

31. Forbes, *100 Years in Golden Gate Park*, 9.

32. "Rollins Named Director of Park Museum," *San Francisco Chronicle*, 13 January 1931, 12. After San Francisco, Rollins went to the Dallas Museum of Art.

33. *San Francisco Chronicle*, 12 July 1931, D8.

34. Alfred Frankenstein, "Heil Plan for Reorganized Museum Told," *San Francisco Chronicle*, 30 December 1934, D3.

35. These changes included hardwood floors in galleries, skylights in corridors, a print room, a library, a textile study room, and an Oriental gallery. *San Francisco Chronicle*, 21 October 1934, D3.

36. *San Francisco Chronicle*, 21 February 1937, 1.

37. Plans were filed by City Architect Dodge A. Riedy, who consulted with Brown and Meyer.

38. Ian McKibbin White, "The Two Fairs," *Apollo* (February 1980): 87.

39. "de Young Director Appointed," *San Francisco Chronicle*, 16 July 1963, 1; "McGregor Leaves Museum Job," *San Francisco Chronicle*, 28 June 1969, 33.

40. Dailey was a prominent San Francisco architect who was best known for his design of modern single-family houses, and who also did large-scale work for the University of California.

CHAPTER 2

1. Barbara Traisman, "After the Earthquake," *Triptych* (January–March 1990): 6–8.

2. Rutherford & Chekene/Structus/Pegasus for the San Francisco Department of Public Works, "Seismic Assessment of Various City-Owned Buildings: M. H. de Young Memorial Museum," November 1992, ES-3.

3. Ellen McGarrahan, "Color it Gone," *San Francisco Weekly*, 4–10 October 1995, 12.

4. Bureau of Architecture, San Francisco Department of Public Works, "Programming Study: M. H. de Young Memorial Museum, California Palace of the Legion of Honor," 30 December 1988.

5. *San Francisco Examiner*, 23 April 1998.

6. *San Francisco Chronicle*, 9 August 1997.

7. *San Francisco Chronicle*, 12 September 1997.

8. David Bonetti, "Reinventing the de Young," *San Francisco Examiner*, 12 October 1997, B-7.

9. Sedway Consulting, "M. H. de Young Memorial Museum: Site Selection Study," June 1997.

10. *San Francisco Examiner*, 8 October 1997.

11. *San Francisco Chronicle*, 18 August 1997.

12. *San Francisco Chronicle*, 18 September 1997.

13. Daniel Zoll, "Moving Violations," *San Francisco Bay Guardian*, 1 October 1997, 10.

14. Carol Kocivar, "Keep the de Young in de Park," *West of Twin Peaks Observer*, October 1997, 7.

15. *San Francisco Chronicle*, 12 June 1997.

16. Interview with Jim Chappell, 26 March 2004.

17. Interview with Harry S. Parker, 7 May 2004.

18. Quoted in Carol Lloyd, "Forever Dede Young: Dede Wilsey is the charismatic driving force behind the expensive de Young Museum," www.sfgate.com/29 September 2004.

19. Interview with Deborah Frieden, 9 April 2004.

20. Nicolai Ouroussoff, "Swiss Treat for Golden Gate Park Art Center," *Los Angeles Times*, 12 June 1999, D1, D11.

21. Interview with Deborah Frieden, 9 April 2004.

22. Jon Carroll, "Bad Ideas Hither and Yon," *San Francisco Chronicle*, 15 June 1999, E12.

23. *San Francisco Chronicle*, 25 June 1999, A2.

24. Ken Alexander, "The new de Young: You Call *That* an Art Museum?" *San Francisco Examiner*, 12 February 2000, D11.

25. *San Francisco Chronicle*, 6 December 2000.

26. Justin Weil, "Critics Take Aim at de Young Rebuild Plan," *Richmond Review*, January 2000.

27. Interview with Jim Chappell, 26 March 2004.

28. Quoted in Ken Coupland, "Aftershock," *Metropolis* (June 2000): 154.

29. *San Francisco Chronicle*, 23 September 1999, A21.

30. *San Francisco Chronicle*, 19 October 1999, A25.

31. Interview with Pam McDonald, 20 February 2004.

32. See Mitchell Schwarzer, "San Francisco in an Age of Reaction," in Edward Robbins and Rodolphe El Khoury, eds., *Shaping the City: Studies in History, Theory and Urban Design* (London: Routledge, 2004), 177–193.

CHAPTER 3

1. Victoria Newhouse, *Towards a New Museum* (New York: Monacelli Press, 1998), 41. Her discussion of Herzog & de Meuron's Goetz Gallery in Munich is accompanied by a photograph of one of their SBB buildings in the Basel railyard, the Depot, next to the Signal Box, which is compared to the gallery in its glazing, 39.

2. Interviews with Harry S. Parker and Diane B Wilsey, San Francisco, 1999–2004.

3. *The Phaidon Atlas of World Architecture* (London: Phaidon, 2004). Only one building in San Francisco, Stanley Saitowitz's Folsom Street Lofts, is listed among the editors' selection of important buildings from the previous five years, whereas 23 Los Angeles buildings were selected.

4. Interviews with Deborah Frieden, San Francisco, 1999–2004.

5. The architectural selection committee for the new de Young museum included Fine Arts Museums of San Francisco trustees: Charles Crocker, Belva Davis, J. Burgess Jamieson, Sylvia Kingsley, Diane Lloyd-Butler, George M. Marcus, Nan Tucker McEvoy, J. Alec Merriam, Barbro Osher, Steven M. Read, and Diane B. Wilsey.

6. Of the eight on the short list, Norman Foster decided he was unable to come to San Francisco for the interview.

7. Interviews with Harrison Fraker, Berkeley, California, 2001–2004.

8. Julia Chance, "The Face of Jacques Herzog," *Architectural Design* 71, no. 6 (November 2001): 48–53.

9. Terence Riley, "Introduction," *Architectures of Herzog & de Meuron* (New York: Peter Blum Edition, 1995), 12–15.

10. See Philip Ursprung, ed., *Herzog & de Meuron: Natural History* (Montreal: Canadian Centre for Architecture/Baden: Lars Muller, 2002).

11. Artists who have worked with Herzog & de Meuron have included: Remy Zaugg, Adrian Schiess, Hannah Villiger, Jeff Wall, Thomas Struth, Helmut Federle, and Pipilotti Rist.

12. Interviews with Jacques Herzog, Pierre de Meuron, Ascan Merganthaler, Harry Gugger, Jean-Frédéric Luscher, Basel, 2004.

13. Riley, *Architectures of Herzog & de Meuron*, 14.

14. Ursprung, *Herzog & de Meuron: Natural History*, 294.

15. Jacques Herzog in an interview with William Curtis, in *El Croquis 109/110: Herzog & de Meuron, 1997–2002* (Madrid: El Croquis, 2004).

16. William Curtis, in ibid., 33.

17. Rowan Moore, et al., *Building Tate Modern* (London: Tate Gallery Publishing, 2000).

18. Interviews with Jacques Herzog, Pierre de Meuron, Ascan Mergenthaler, Harry Gugger, Jean-Frédéric Luscher, Basel, 2004.

19. Interviews with Pierre de Meuron, Basel and San Francisco, 1999–2004.

20. See Brian O'Doherty, *Inside the White Cube: The Ideology of Gallery Space* (Santa Monica: Lapis Press, 1988).

21. *San Francisco Chronicle*, 11 June 1999, A1.

22. Jon Carroll, "Bad Ideas Hither and Yon," *San Francisco Chronicle*, 15 June 1999, E12.

23. "Herzog & de Meuron 1998–2002," 33–49.

SELECTED BIBLIOGRAPHY

CHAPTER 1

California Architect and Building News 9 and 10 (September–October 1893).

California Midwinter International Exposition Guide and Souvenir. San Francisco: Whitcher, Allen & Boldemann, [1894].

California Midwinter International Exposition: The Official History. San Francisco: 1894.

Chandler, Arthur, and Marvin Nathan. *The Fantastic Fair: The Story of the California Midwinter International Exposition, Golden Gate Park, San Francisco, 1894.* St. Paul: Pogo Press, 1993.

Clark, Robert Judson. "Louis Christian Mullgardt and the Court of the Ages." *Journal of the Society of Architectural Historians* 21, no. 4 (December 1962): 171–178.

_____. "The Life and Architectural Accomplishment of Louis Christian Mullgardt (1866–1942)." Master's thesis, Stanford University, June 1964.

Clary, Raymond H. *The Making of Golden Gate Park, the Early Years: 1865–1906.* San Francisco: A California Living Book, 1980.

Colburn, Frona Eunice Wait. "The Things of Substance in Wishing Land." *Overland Monthly* 87, no. 1 (January 1929): 19, 25.

Corbett, Michael R. "An Architectural History of the M. H. de Young Memorial Museum, Golden Gate Park, San Francisco." Report prepared for the Fine Arts Museums of San Francisco.

Driscoll, Marjorie C. *The M. H. de Young Memorial Museum.* San Francisco: The Park Commission, 1921.

Executive Committee of the California Midwinter International Exposition. *Guide to the Halls and Galleries of the Memorial Museum Purchased with Surplus Proceeds of the California Midwinter International Exposition by the Executive Committee.* San Francisco: H. S. Crocker Company, 1895.

_____. *The Official History of the California Midwinter International Exposition, A Descriptive Record of the Origin, Development and Success of the Great Industrial Expositional Enterprise, Held in San Francisco from January to July 1894.* San Francisco: H. S. Crocker Company, 1895.

Forbes, Pamela, ed. *100 Years in Golden Gate Park: A Pictorial History of the M. H. de Young Memorial Museum.* San Francisco: The Fine Arts Museums of San Francisco, 1995.

Huson, Willis E. "The Memorial Museum at Golden Gate Park." *The Western Architect* 27 (December 1918): 127–128; plates 8–10.

Leonard, A. T., Jr. "In Memoriam: George Haviland Barron, 1869–1942." *California Historical Society Quarterly* 21 (December 1942): 378–379.

"Memorial Museum, Golden Gate Park, San Francisco, California: Louis Christian Mullgardt, Architect." *Architectural Review* 12, no. 2 (February 1921): plates 19–20.

Midwinter Fair and the Golden State: Art Views, California, Educational Series No. 1, March 26, 1894. San Francisco, H. S. Crocker Company, 1894.

Millard, Bailey. *History of the San Francisco Bay Region.* 2 vols. Chicago: American Historical Society, 1924.

Morrow, Irving F. "Memorial Museum, Golden Gate Park, San Francisco." *The Building Review* 17 (August 1919): 26, plates 19–24.

_____. "Louis Christian Mullgardt, 1876–1942." *Architect and Engineer* 148 (February 1942): 42–43.

Mullgardt, Louis Christian. *The Architecture and Landscape Gardening of the Exposition.* San Francisco: Paul Elder and Company, 1915.

"Mute Witness to Vanished Cultures & Wilcomb's Indian Collections." *Museum of California* 3, no. 7 (January 1980): 4–5.

Newcomb, Rexford. "The Work of Louis Christian Mullgardt in Honolulu." *Western Architect* 31 (November 1922): 123–126.

Pollock, Christopher. *Golden Gate Park: San Francisco's Urban Oasis in Vintage Postcards.* San Francisco: Arcadia Publishing, 2003.

Roberts, Edwards. "Some Architectural Effects." *Overland Monthly,* Midwinter Fair Number, 23, no. 136 (April 1894): 341–351.

San Francisco Chronicle

"Unity of Action; Problems of the Winter Fair; Work on the Site to Begin Soon." 17 July 1893, 2.

"Ready to Begin. Building Plans Wanted Immediately . . . A Call to Local Artists and Architects . . . Outlining What the Five Main Structures of the Midwinter Fair Are to Be." 18 July 1893, 8.

"The Midwinter Fair . . . Waiting for Ground to be Broken." 15 August 1893, 10.

"Fine Arts Building, Pronounced by Art Critics the Prettiest Structure of the Fair . . . McDougall's Masterpiece." 31 December 1893, entire issue.

O'Shaughnessy, M. M. "The Building and the Laying Out of the Midwinter Fair." 28 January 1894, 40.

"Oakland Museum Curator is Dead: C. P. Wilcomb Assembled the Golden Gate Park Collection." 24 June 1915.

"M. H. de Young Explains Memorial Museum Plans." 24 September 1916, 37.

"Cornerstone of Memorial Museum to Be Laid Today." 15 April 1917, 57.

"Park Museum Curator Goes to Final Rest." 3 November 1917, 10.

"New Curator in Charge at Park Museum; Charles E. Penez Assumes His Duties as Successor to late William Altman." 5 December 1917, 10.

"New Memorial Museum Unit Will Be Opened Today." 22 February 1919, 11.

"John W. Rogers, Supervisors' Chief Assistant Aid, Drops Dead at City Hall." 15 July 1930, 3.

"Rollins Named Director of Park Museum; Trustees of De Young Galleries Fill Post Vacant Since 1925." 13 January 1931, 12.

"The New Museum." 1 March 1931, picture section, 5.

"Opening of Museum Wing Nears." 12 July 1931, D8.

"Park Museum Changes Made." 21 October 1934, D3.

Frankenstein, Alfred. "Heil Plan for Reorganized Museum Told." 30 December 1934, D3.

"De Young Museum Occupies Enlarged Quarters." 21 February 1937, 1.

"de Young Director Appointed." 16 July 1963, 1.

"McGregor Leaves Museum Job." 28 June 1969, 33.

San Francisco Park Commission. *The M. H. de Young Memorial Museum, Golden Gate Park, San Francisco . . . The Story of its Foundation and the Object of its Founder.* San Francisco: San Francisco City and County, 1921.

"Some Recent California Architecture: The Work of Louis Christian Mullgardt, Architect." *Architectural Forum* 33 (August 1920): 51–54.

Stretch, Cynthia. "Chronological List of Changes to the M. H. de Young Memorial Museum." Prepared for the Archives of the Fine Arts Museums of San Francisco, 28 August 1987.

Strother, W. M. "Facts About the M. H. de Young Memorial Museum." 31 December 1935.

Taber, I. W. *The "Monarch" Souvenir of Sunset City and Sunset Scenes; Being Views of California Midwinter Fair and Famous Scenes in the Golden State, Pacific Coast Educational Series, Portfolio no. 1–15.* San

Francisco: H. S. Crocker, 1894.

University of California at Santa Barbara Art Gallery and M. H. de Young Memorial Museum. *Louis Christian Mullgardt, 1866–1942.* Catalogue of an exhibition marking the centennial year of the architect's birth. Santa Barbara: University of California/San Francisco: M. H. de Young Memorial Museum, 1966.

Valentiner, William R. "The Museum of Tomorrow," 656–674. In Paul Zucker, ed. *New Architecture and City Planning.* New York: Philosophical Library, 1944.

White, Ian McKibbin. "The Two Fairs." *Apollo* (February 1980): 86–89.

Young, Terence. *Building San Francisco's Parks, 1850–1930.* Baltimore: Johns Hopkins University Press, 2004.

CHAPTERS 2–5

Ackerman, Hans Christophe. "Basel's Cabinets of Art and Curiosities in the 16th and 17th Centuries." In Oliver Impey and Arthur MacGregor, eds. *The Origins of Museums.* Oxford: Clarendon Press, 1985.

Betsky, Aaron. "Swiss Reserve." *Architecture* 87, no. 6 (June 1998): 122–127.

Bonetti, David. "Reinventing the de Young." *San Francisco Examiner,* 12 October 1997, B-7.

Brasch, Marianne. "Herzog & de Meuron." *Fragen zur Architecture.* Basel: Birkhauser Verlag, 1995.

Bureau of Architecture, San Francisco Department of Public Works. "Programming Study: M. H. de Young Memorial Museum, California Palace of the Legion of Honor." 30 December 1988.

Carroll, Jon. "Bad Ideas Hither and Yon." *San Francisco Chronicle,* 15 June 1999, E12.

Chance, Julia. "The Face of Jacques Herzog." *Architectural Design* 71, no. 6 (November 2001): 48–53.

Coolidge, John. *Patrons and Architects: Designing Museums in the Twentieth Century.* Fort Worth: University of Texas Press, 1989.

Coupland, Ken. "Aftershock." *Metropolis* (June 2000): 154.

Curtis, William J. R. "Herzog & de Meuron's New Tate Gallery of Modern Art." *Architectural Record* (June 2000): 103.

Davidson, Cynthia. "An Interview with Herzog & de Meuron." *ANY* 13 (1996).

El Croquis 60/84: Herzog & de Meuron, 1993–1997. Madrid: El Croquis, 2000.

El Croquis 109/110: Herzog & de Meuron, 1997–2002. Madrid: El Croquis, 2004.

Hamlin, Jesse. "Earthquake Warning for de Young." *San Francisco Chronicle,* 14 January 1993, D1, D3.

_____. "The de Young Museum's Temporary Quake Fix." *San Francisco Chronicle,* 9 April 1993.

Herzog & de Meuron. Basel: Architecture Museum Basel and Editions Weise, 1989.

Herzog, Jacques. "Jacques Herzog: Recent Work of Herzog & de Meuron." *Columbia Documents of Architecture* 4 (1995).

_____, and Pierre de Meuron. *Architektur Denkform.* Basel: Architekturmuseum Basel, 1989.

_____. *Herzog & de Meuron.* Barcelona: Editorial Gustavo Gill, 1989.

_____. "The Hidden Geometry of Nature." *Quaderns* 181/182 (1989).

_____. "Two fields of Operation: Surfaces and Structures." *Lotus* 76 (1993).

Hood, Walter. *Urban Diaries.* Washington, D.C.: Spacemaker, 1997.

Huber, Dorothee. "The Hidden and the Apparent: Comments on the Work of H & de M." In Wilfried Wang, ed. *Herzog & de Meuron.* Zurich: Artemis Verlag, 1992.

Huxtable, Ada Louise. *Making Architecture: The Getty Center.* Los Angeles: The Getty Trust, 1997.

Ketcham, Diana. "Will the Caged Rock Fly in Napa." *New York Times,* 21 May 1998, E1–2.

Kocivar, Carol. "Keep the de Young in de Park." *West of Twin Peaks Observer,* October 1997, 7.

Koolhaas, Rem. "New Discipline." *Arch-Plus* 129/130 (September 1985).

Kuhnert, Niklaus. "Herzog, Jacques, and Pierre de Meuron: Minimalism and Ornament." *ARCH+* 120/130 (1995).

Lloyd, Carol. "Forever Dede Young: Dede Wilsey is the charismatic driving force behind the expensive de Young Museum." www.sfgate.com/29 September 2004.

Loos, Adolf. *Ornament Is Crime.* Innsbruck: Trotzdem, 1930.

Lucan, Pierre. "Vers une Architecture." *DU* 5 (1992).

Mack, Gerhard. *Herzog & de Meuron Complete Works, 1978–1988.* Basel: Birkhauser Verlag, 1996.

_____. *Herzog & de Meuron Complete Works, 1989–1991.* Basel: Birkhauser Verlag, 1997.

_____. *Herzog & de Meuron Complete Works, 1992–1996.* Basel: Birkhauser Verlag, 2005.

_____, and Valeria Liebermann. *Herzog & de Meuron: Eberswalde Library.* London: Architectural Association, 2000.

The Making of a Modern Museum: The San Francisco Museum of Modern Art. San Francisco: San Francisco Museum of Modern Art, 1994.

McGarrahan, Ellen. "Color it Gone." *San Francisco Weekly,* 4–10 October 1995, 12.

Moneo, Rafael. "Foreword." In Wilfried Wang, ed. *Herzog & de Meuron Buildings and Projects, 1982–1990.* New York: Rizzoli, 1990.

_____. "In Celebration of Matter." *AV Monografias* 77 (1999): 22.

Moore, Rowan, and Raymund Ryan, with contributions by Adrian Hardwicke and Gavin Stamp. *Building Tate Modern: Herzog & de Meuron Transforming Giles Gilbert Scott.* London: Tate Gallery Publishing, 2000.

Newhouse, Victoria. *Towards a New Museum.* New York: Monacelli Press, 1998.

O'Doherty, Brian. *Inside the White Cube: The Ideology of Gallery Space.* Santa Monica: Lapis Press, 1988.

Ouroussoff, Nicolai. "Swiss Treat for Golden Gate Park Art Center." *Los Angeles Times,* 12 June 1999, D1, D11.

The Phaidon Atlas of World Architecture. London: Phaidon, 2004.

Prada Aoyama Tokyo: Herzog & de Meuron. Milan: Fondazione Prada, 2003.

Riley, Terence. *Light Construction.* New York: The Museum of Modern Art, 1995.

_____. *The Un-private House.* New York: The Museum of Modern Art, 1999.

_____, ed. *Architectures of Herzog & de Meuron.* New York: Peter Blum Edition, 1995.

Rutherford & Chekene/Structus/Pegasus for the San Francisco Department of Public Works. "Seismic Assessment of Various City-Owned Buildings: M. H. de Young Memorial Museum." November 1992, ES-3.

Ryan, Raymund. "Material Worlds and the Fabricated Landscape." *Blueprint* 123 (1995).

San Francisco Chronicle, 1997–1999.

San Francisco Examiner, 1997–1998.

Schmertz, Mildred. "luxe, calme, et volupté: Renzo Piano's Fondation Beyeler." *Architectural Digest* (October 1997): 94–106.

Schwarzer, Mitchell. "San Francisco in an Age of Reaction." In Edward Robbins and Rodolphe El Khoury, eds. *Shaping the City: Studies in History, Theory and Urban Design.* London: Routledge, 2004, 177–193.

Searing, Helen. *New American Art Museums.* New York: Whitney Museum of American Art/Berkeley: University of California Press, 1982.

Sedway Consulting. "M. H. de Young Memorial Museum: Site Selection Study." June 1997.

"Tate Modern." *The Art Magazine* 21 (2000).

"Tate Modern by Herzog & de Meuron." *Du* 706 (May 2000).

Traisman, Barbara. "After the Earthquake." *Triptych* (January–March 1990): 6–8.

Ursprung. Philip, ed. *Herzog & de Meuron: Natural History.* Montreal: Canadian Centre for Architecture/Baden: Lars Muller, 2002.

Vischer, Theodora. *Herzog & de Meuron Drawings.* New York: Peter Blum Edition, 1997.

_____. "Interview with Jacques Herzog." In Wilfried Wang, ed. *Herzog & de Meuron Buildings and Projects, 1982–1990.* New York: Rizzoli, 1990.

_____. "Interviews with Jacques Herzog and Thomas Ruff." In Terence Riley, ed. *Architectures of Herzog & de Meuron.* New York: Peter Blum Edition, 1994.

Volkart, Yvonne. "Giving a Glow to a Given Place." *Flash Art International* 185 (1995).

Wang, Wilfried. *Herzog & de Meuron.* Basel: Birkhauser Verlag, 1998.

_____, ed. *Herzog & de Meuron.* Zurich: Artemis Verlag, 1992.

_____, ed. *Herzog & de Meuron Buildings and Projects, 1982–1990.* New York: Rizzoli, 1990.

Weil, Justin. "Critics Take Aim at de Young Rebuild Plan." *Richmond Review,* January 2000.

Karen S. and Frank J. Caufield
Chevron Corporation
Robert S. Colman
Mr. and Mrs. Newton A. Cope
David L. Davies and John D. Weeden
Mr. and Mrs. Reid W. Dennis
Rajnikant and Helen Desai
The Family of Richard Diebenkorn
Carol and Dixon R. Doll
The Charles D. and Frances K.
    Field Fund
Frances K. and Charles D. Field
    Foundation
Fleishhacker Foundation
Fritz Family Foundation
Gap Foundation
Lisa and Douglas Goldman Fund
Mr. and Mrs. Andrew J. Goodman
Sallie and Dick Griffith
Richard and Beatrice Hagopian
Mary Gary Harrison Trust
Lenore and Frank Heffernan
Gladys L. Hoefer
Jacqueline and Peter Hoefer
George and Beverly James
The JEC Foundation
Dorothy and Bradford Jeffries
Sylvia and Leonard Kingsley
Mr. and Mrs. William E. Larkin
Doris Shoong and Theodore B. Lee
Betty Lou Levin
Fred M. and Nancy Livingston Levin,
    The Shenson Foundation, in
    memory of Drs. Ben and A. Jess
    Shenson
Emily Prettyman Lowell
The Henry Luce Foundation, Inc.
Mrs. Robert A. Magowan
Mr. and Mrs. Archibald McClure
Caroline McCoy-Jones
The Eugene McDermott Foundation
Lorna F. Meyer and Dennis M. Calas
Michael and Patricia O'Neill
Kenneth Rainin
Pamela and Richard Rigg
John Henry Samter
The San Francisco Foundation
The Shorenstein Family
Laurence L. Spitters
Martha and William Steen
William Arba Stimson
In memory of Wycliffe G. Sweet
William Laney Thornton and
    Pasha Dritt Thornton
U.S. Department of Housing and
    Urban Development
Volunteer Council of the
    Fine Arts Museums
Robert T. Wall Family
Will K. Weinstein
Judy and Brayton Wilbur
Nick, Shannon, Rory Wilsey
Zellerbach Family Foundation

**FAMILY ROOM DONORS TO THE
NEW DE YOUNG FUND**

Anonymous
Rachael Balyeat
The Eva Benson Buck Charitable Trust
Nora P. and George C. Chen
Mr. and Mrs. George W. Coombe, Jr.
Louise M. Davies Foundation
Burnham and Nina Enersen
Mr. and Mrs. Milo S. Gates
Ann and Gordon Getty Foundation
William G. Gilmore Foundation
Eugene H. Gray and Stephanie S. Gray
Mr. and Mrs. Edward M. Griffith
Gruber Family Foundation
Dr. Yorke and Jacqueline Jacobson
Effiellen Jeffries
Mr. and Mrs. Peter M. Joost
Barbara and Ron Kaufman
Mr. and Mrs. Jude P. Laspa
Lamar Leland
Mr. and Mrs. E. Rust Muirhead
Virginia Patterson
Constance C. Peabody
The Morris Stulsaft Foundation
Roselyne Chroman Swig
Mr. and Mrs. Joseph O. Tobin II
The Samuel Untermyer Charitable
    Remainder Unitrust
William E. Weiss Foundation, Inc.
Willis Lease Finance Corporation
Mr. and Mrs. R. Martin Wiskemann
Mr. and Mrs. Donald L. Wyler

The Acacia Foundation in memory
    of John M. Webb
Achenbach Graphic Arts Council
    of the Fine Arts Museums
Vanda and Jose Alicastro
Daphne and Bart Araujo
Martha and Bruce Atwater
In memory of Madeleine Baaba
Charles W. Banta
Ann Fay Barry
Jeanne D. Benatar
Cynthia S. and Gary F. Bengier
Mrs. Geraldine Grace Benoist
Mr. and Mrs. Kenneth G. Berry
David A. Blanton III
Kimberly and Simon Blattner
Donald and Wanda Blockhus
Peter Boesch and Darril Hudson
Barbara Lee Boucke
Ann S. Bowers
Jamie and Philip Bowles Family
Daphne and Bob Bransten
Harold and Ava Jean Brumbaum
Cahan & Associates
Shirley and Dick Cahill Fund
Barbara and John Callander
Frank and Patricia Carrubba
Donald and Carole Chaiken
Iris S. Chan and Michael Chan

Claudio Chiuchiarelli Family
    Foundation
Drs. Stephen R. Chun and
    Doris Sze Chun
Mr. and Mrs. A. W. Clausen
Walter and Peggy Clemens
John Philip Coghlan
Cornelia Myers Cogsdell
Ernest and Susan Collins
John T. and Katherine S. Collins
Mr. and Mrs. Terrence E. Comerford
Edward and Nancy Conner
Ransom and Nan Cook
Carol Gray Costigan
In memory of Thomas B. Crowley, Sr.
Stephen and Jean Cuff
Mrs. Robert Danforth
Suzanne and Mark Darley
Daughters of Penelope Foundation Inc.
Mr. and Mrs. Walter Edwin Dean II
Mr. and Mrs. Charles C. de Limur
Mrs. Gunther R. Detert
Nicole and Gaylord Dillingham
Princess Ranieri di San Faustino
Isabelle Z. Dokouzian
Joan D. Donlon
Mrs. Morris M. Doyle
Mr. and Mrs. Myron Du Bain
Christina Duvaras
East Bay Auxiliary of the Fine Arts
    Museums
Delia Fleishhacker Ehrlich
Lexie and Bob Ellsworth
Jacqueline and Christian P. Erdman
Marion and Jack Euphrat
Roger L. Evans
Emily Huggins Fine
Mrs. James Flood
Fong & Chan Architects (FCA)
Marcia L. Forman
Barbara E. Foster
Carlo S. and Dianne A. Fowler
Donald Frediani and Renata Gasperi
The Robert and Michelle Friend
    Foundation
Mr. and Mrs. Dean Frisbie
Mr. and Mrs. Launce E. Gamble
Anna G. Gardner
Dr. and Mrs. Joseph R. Goldyne
Dr. and Mrs. Robert B. Gordon
Phyllis and Eugene Gottfried
Harriet and Maurice Gregg
Donald M. Gregory, Jr.
Elisabeth E. Griffinger
Dr. Gerold M. and Kayla W. Grodsky
Mr. and Mrs. H. I. Grousbeck
Michael Hackett and Tracy Freedman
Margaret Alice and
    Joseph Harvey Harris, M.D.
Jessica Ely Hart
Charlene Harvey
Dr. and Mrs. Jun Hatoyama
Molly O'Conor Hauser
Mr. and Mrs. Richard Heafey

Elaine Henderson
Mrs. Louis E. Hendricks
Benjamin J. Henley, Jr.
Jane and Glenn Hickerson
Bill Hilliard and Heather Schultz
Mr. and Mrs. Austin E. Hills
Hillsborough Auxiliary of the
    Fine Arts Museums
Dr. Gloria Hing in memory of Mary
    and Wy C. Hing
William D. Hobi and Soojung Ko
Jan and Maurice Holloway
Adrienne Horn and Stephen Horn II
The George Hornstein Family
    Foundation
Elinor F. Howenstine
Donna Ewald Huggins and
    Charles N. Huggins
Leslie and George Hume
Derk and Fredericka Hunter
Mr. and Mrs. John N. Hunter
Mamoru and Yasuko Inouye
Esther Jennings
Katharine Hotchkis Johnson
Amy Edwards Jordan
The Juffali Family in memory
    of Joseph Martin, Jr.
Mr. and Mrs. Fritz F. Kasten
Mr. and Mrs. James P. Kelly
Susan Gray and Arthur Kern
June Hope Kingsley
Robert and Dorothy Kissick
Mr. and Mrs. Clarence E. Knapp
Marian S. Kobayashi
Joyce M. Konigsberg honoring
    her parents, Merle and William
    Konigsberg
Mr. and Mrs. Charles S. LaFollette
The Landreth Family
Mr. and Mrs. Carter L. Larsen
Marsha and Michael Lasky
Sandra and John D. Leland, Jr.
Mr. and Mrs. Edmund W. Littlefield
Diane B. Lloyd-Butler and Thomas
    O. Lloyd-Butler
Ruthanne and Dixon Long
Josephine Caffese Lott
Fern and Bill Lowenberg
Mr. and Mrs. Charles F. Lowrey
James J. and Eileen D. Ludwig
Stephanie and William MacColl
Mr. and Mrs. Richard B. Madden
In memory of Delores C. Malone,
    Executive Secretary Emerita
Charlene C. and Tom F. Marsh Family
Harvey and Eve Masonek
Alicia McEvoy
Mr. and Mrs. J. Frank McGinnis
Mr. and Mrs. James C. McIntosh
Mr. and Mrs. Andrew C. McLaughlin III
Burt and Deedee McMurtry
Mr. and Mrs. James K. McWilliams
Alexander R. Mehran
Mendelson Family Fund

Bailey and Chris Meyer
Byron R. Meyer
G.H.C. Meyer Family Foundation
A. E. and Martha Michelbacher Fund
    of Marin Community Foundation
Bruce and Adrienne Mitchell
Gladyne K. Mitchell
Tina and Hamid Moghadam
Martin Muller
Nancy and Tim Muller
Al H. Nathe
National Council of the Fine Arts Museums
Nancy E. Nebeker
Dorothy Ann and Howard Nelson
Ellen M. and Walter S. Newman
Mr. and Mrs. John Nichols
Winifred and Morris Noble
In memory of Claude Oakland, FAIA
Mr. and Mrs. Peter J. O'Hara
Nancy Suzanne Olson
John S. Osterweis
Joy Ou
David T. Owsley
The Charles Page Family
Jean and James Palmer and Family
Joan Ramsay Palmer
Ellen and Harry Parker
The Parker Family Foundation
Wendy and Fred Parkin
Mr. and Mrs. Warren W. Perry
Mr. and Mrs. W. Robert Phillips
Lisa and Jay Pierrepont
Tony Price and Connie Cox Price
Gerald W. Purmal and M. Jean
    Gundlach Purmal
Genelle Relfe
The Paul and Louise Renne Family
Venetta and John Rohal
Family of Leslie L. Roos
Joan and Robert Rorick
Mr. and Mrs. Claude Rosenberg, Jr.
Toby and Sally Rosenblatt
Henriette Rothenberg
Kate and George W. Rowe
W. Timothy and Annette Ryan
Prentice and Paul Sack
Salvatore Ferragamo
San Francisco Ceramic Circle
    of the Fine Arts Museums
Florence and Sam Scarlett
Mr. and Mrs. J. David Schemel
Sande Lange Schlumberger
Gary Schnitzer and Sandra
    Wilder-Schnitzer
Randee and Joseph Seiger
Mr. and Mrs. Edwin A. Seipp, Jr.
Gail P. Seneca
Mr. and Mrs. H. Boyd Seymour
J. Gary and O. J. Shansby Foundation
Dr. A. Jess Shenson
The Shifting Foundation
Gerald and Donna Silverberg
Matthew and Ellen Simmons Family
Kathleen A. Skeels

Cynthia Inaba, Coordinator of School
Programs
Eileen Lew Morris, Coordinator
of Family Programs
Emily Doman, Research Assistant

Publications and Graphic Design
Ann Heath Karlstrom, Director
of Publications and Graphic Design
Elisa Urbanelli, Managing Editor

Ron Rick, Chief Graphic and
Electronic Signage Designer
Juliana Pennington, Senior Graphic
Designer
Christine McCullough, Graphics Buyer
and Production Manager
Martha Crawford, Graphic Designer –
New de Young Project

Exhibitions
Krista Davis, Director of Exhibitions
Allison Satre, Exhibitions Assistant

Exhibitions: Technical Production
Bill White, Director of Exhibition and
Technical Production
Richard Biernacki, Chief Museum
Technician
Robert Haycock, Principal Museum
Technician
William Huggins, Lighting Designer
Virginia Kelly, Technical Production
Manager
Mark Garrett, Senior Museum
Technician
Rick Wilds, Senior Museum
Technician
Virginia Benavidez, Museum
Technician
Lynn Goodman, Museum Technician
Arie Knoops, Museum Technician
Paul Palacios, Museum Technician

New de Young Project
Lucia Coronel, Architectural and
Design Associate
Adalberto Castrillon, Museum
Technician
Camille Duplantier, Museum
Technician/Mountmaker
Kevin W. Evensen, Museum Technician
Howard H. Faxon, Museum Technician
Mark Grim, Museum Technician
Osvaldo Ruiz, Museum Technician
Tilroe Stevenson, Museum Technician

Project Funded Museum Technicians
Don Larson
Kent M. Middleton
Nancy Mintz
David Sullivan
Paul Tavian
Brian Weinstein

DEVELOPMENT

Barbara Boucke, Deputy Director
for Development and Membership
Anne-Marie Bonfilio, Director
of Corporate Relations and Capital
Campaign Associate
Gerry Chow, Senior Grants Officer
Emily Leach, Director of Individual
Giving
Marcia Davey, Manager, Museum
Support Groups Travel
Mary Craig Tennile, Development
and Information Systems Manager
Matt Leffert, Development Associate,
Annual Support
Jessica Turner, Development Associate,
Donor Fulfillment
Victoria Ricciarelli, Development
Coordinator

Membership Services
Gina Tan, Director of Membership
and Annual Fund
Elizabeth (Betty) Sommerfeld,
Assistant Membership Director
Norah K. McKinney, Membership
Office Manager
Elaine H. Chang, Database
Management Specialist
Gail Jarocki, Database Management
Specialist
Jeff Petrie, Membership Programs and
Publications Coordinator
Anne Chao, Membership
Services Clerk
Sean Mason, Membership
Services Clerk
Marilyn Langston, Membership
Services Clerk
Christopher Lux, Membership
Services Clerk

BUDGET AND FINANCE

Stephen Dykes, Deputy Director for
Budget and Finance

Accounting
Robert Cullison, Controller
Brian Marston, Assistant Controller –
Information Systems, Purchasing,
and Special Projects
Simon Chiu, Principal Accountant
Angeline K. Shin, Principal Payroll
and Personnel Clerk
Olivia Xuetao Jiang, Senior Accounts
Clerk
Daiquiri Weed, Senior Accounts Clerk
Ellen Sanchez, Accounts Clerk

Fine Arts Museums Foundation
Michele Gutierrez, Fiscal Officer
Frances F. Escobar, Clerk

OPERATIONS AND PERSONNEL

Debbie Albuquerque, Deputy Director
for Operations and Personnel

Admissions
Erlinda Cruz, Cashier
Gayatri Kishore, Cashier
Yan W. Lee, Cashier
Un C. Lei, Cashier

Engineering
James N. Hartman, Building and
Grounds Maintenance
Superintendent
Michael C. Badger, Senior Stationary
Engineer
Michael J. Richards, Senior Stationary
Engineer
Altaf Bhatti, Stationary Engineer
Anatoliy Kalika, Stationary Engineer

Operations Support Group
Sherin S. Kyte, Legion Administrator
Allan Barna, Health and Safety
Technician
Annette Holmes, Operations
Coordinator
Christopher Huson, Museum Courier

Audio Visual Technicians
Kali Boyce
Cecily Chow
Val Chow
Michael Golds
Sean Mason
Carol Oliva
Richard Rice

Facility Rental
Sibyl Graham, Facility Rental
Coordinator and Auxiliary Support
Bernard Cummings, Jr., Events
Assistant
Tracy Denham, Events Assistant
Brooke Scallion, Events Assistant
Alice Schmidt, Events Assistant
Doris Teller, Events Assistant

Security
David Dippel, Lead Museum Security
Supervisor
Kevin C. Allen, Museum Security
Supervisor
Albert G. deGuzman, Museum
Security Supervisor
Paul A. Kahn, Museum Security
Supervisor
Elaine Low, Museum Security
Supervisor
Karl Schumann, Museum Security
Supervisor

Museum Guards
Rosa M. Alvarez
Jose R. Cenit
Maria Teresa T. Cenit
Jane E. Coffey
Arturo G. Collado
Michael W. Duffy
Domingo B. Espadilla
Benjamin S. Factor
Nenita J. Fleming
Robert M. Galicia
Leonard Gallard
Richard Isom
Christopher L. Kirby
Paula Kotakis
David K. Martinez
Gerald P. Meisel
Ardern L. Mynhier
Nestor C. Naval
Barry Rodriguez
Rebecca Rosewicz
Carlos C. Sanchez
Ricardo Serrano
James Thomas
Serafin A. Tiomico
Biagio Torrano
Nerissa B. Torquido
Rafael Valiente
Quirino C. Viray
Monica Whitley
Robert Wilcox
Sam K. Woo
Don Wood

Security Guards
Leora Anderson
Jeffrey B. Atanacio
Trina D. Bell
James N. Boland
Gina J. Cuneo
Teresa I. Davis
Guimy Etheart
Shawn Farrell
Richard C. Johnson
Yin Myo Kaung
Gimli L. Klein
Linda F. Madero
John J. Matanguihan
Erika N. Miller
Howard L. Mitchell, Jr
Cristina G. Mooney
James M. Motley
Eugenia E. Ng
Darwin T. Ragland
Shahrukh A. Rizvi
Andrea L. Scott-Finney
Lorenzo Serrano
Otis L. Stroman
Marina M. Telias
Larry K. Toji
Boris Veynberg
Talbert H. Webb
Ineva J. Williams
Darwin Wong

Volunteer and Visitor Services
Marilyn Duffy-McClellan, Volunteer
and Visitor Services Manager
Tish Brown, Disability and Public
Safety Assistant
Donna Duncan, Switchboard Operator
Barbara Giffen, Switchboard Operator
Nina Lazareva, Visitor Services
Attendant
Myongja Park, Visitor Services
Attendant
Lupe Virgen, Visitor Services
Attendant

MARKETING AND COMMUNICATIONS

Carolyn Macmillan, Deputy Director
for Marketing and Communications
Chaney Rankin, Marketing and
Communications Assistant –
New de Young

Media Relations and Advertising
Linda Katona, Director of Advertising
and Promotion
Barbara Traisman, Senior Media
Relations Officer
Wendy Norris, Communications
Officer – New de Young
Andrew Fox, Marketing and
Communications Assistant

de Young Museum Store
Stuart Hata, General Manager
Timothy Niedert, Book Buyer
Rose Desuyo Burke, Buyer
Kelly Chin, Buying Assistant

Legion of Honor Museum Store
Couric Payne, General Manager
Nick Romero, Lead Sales Associate
Jennie Politis, Sales Clerk
John Varnado, Sales Clerk

Museum Stores Warehouse
Thomas J. Tripoli, Assistant to the
Managers for Receiving and
Fulfillment
Luke Boyd, Receiving and Fulfillment
Clerk

As of 31 May 2005

ACKNOWLEDGMENTS

Diana Ketcham

The creation of a book, like the creation of a building, is a miracle of teamwork and timing. This book would not have been possible without the contributions of Michael R. Corbett, Mitchell Schwarzer, and Aaron Betsky; and architect Jacques Herzog and landscape architect Walter Hood, who were eloquent commentators on their own work. For the accounts of the years of institutional planning and community discussion that accompanied the design of the new de Young, this book is especially indebted to new de Young project director Deborah Frieden, Harrison Fraker of the College of Environmental Design at the University of California at Berkeley, Jim Chappell of San Francisco Planning and Urban Research (SPUR), and the members of the Fine Arts Museums building committee, in particular board president Diane B. Wilsey and museum director Harry S. Parker III.

The description of Herzog & de Meuron's design approach relies on interviews in Basel with architects Jacques Herzog, Pierre de Meuron, Ascan Mergenthaler, Harry Gugger, and Jean-Frédéric Luscher. Jayne Barlow added her valuable perspective from Herzog & de Meuron's San Francisco office. Nuno Lopez contributed his understanding of the work of Fong & Chan Architects in San Francisco, and Bill Zahner of the facade work by his family firm, A. Zahner Company, in Kansas City. Cherise Chen Moueix and Pam and Dick Kramlich shared their experiences as California clients of Herzog & de Meuron. I am indebted to Andrew Hoyem for his elucidation of design problems large and small, to Helene Prentice of the College of Enviromental Design for her knowledge of research sources, and to Stuart Gunn for editorial assistance.

The challenge of photographing an unfinished building produced extraordinary results by architectural photographer Mark Darley, assisted by Radek Skrivanek and James Thomas. Additional photography was supplied by Kaz Tsuruta. On the construction site, Jim Roux was an invaluable guide.

Others from the Fine Arts Museums staff contributed their time and expertise: Bahiyyih Watson, Patricia Lacson, Suzy Peterson, Judy Gough, Andrew Fox, Ron Rick, Lauren Ito, and Wendy Norris. Esther Zumsteg, Danica Willi, and Beate Quasching at the Herzog & de Meuron Basel office were helpful in numerous ways. At Thames & Hudson, I wish to thank: Jamie Camplin, Mark Lane, Sarah Praill, Anna Bennett, and Jane Cutter in London; and Susan Dwyer in New York.

Special recognition is owed to Ann Karlstrom and Elisa Urbanelli of the Fine Arts Museums Publications Department for their dedication and unflagging good humor through the complex process of making these diverse contributions into a book.

INDEX

208